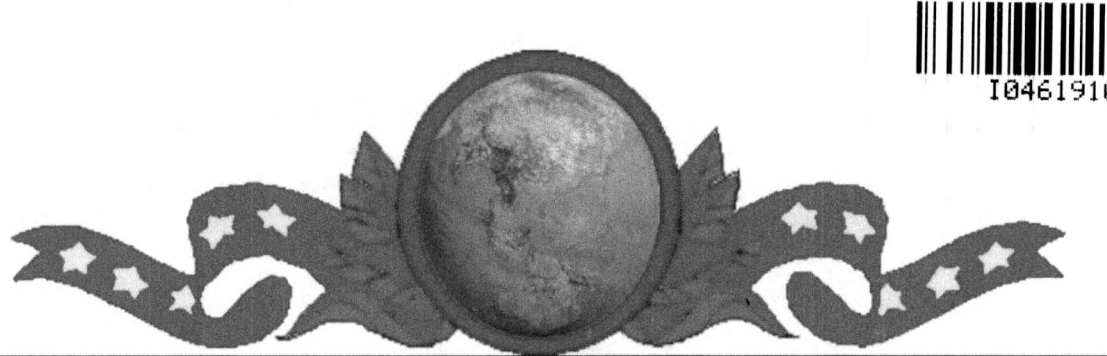

Real World
Colouring Book
For Advanced Users & Adults

Copyright 2019 By John Boom

50 Images
Created From Real Life Photos
For You To Colour As You Please.

ISBN 978-0-359-76564-5

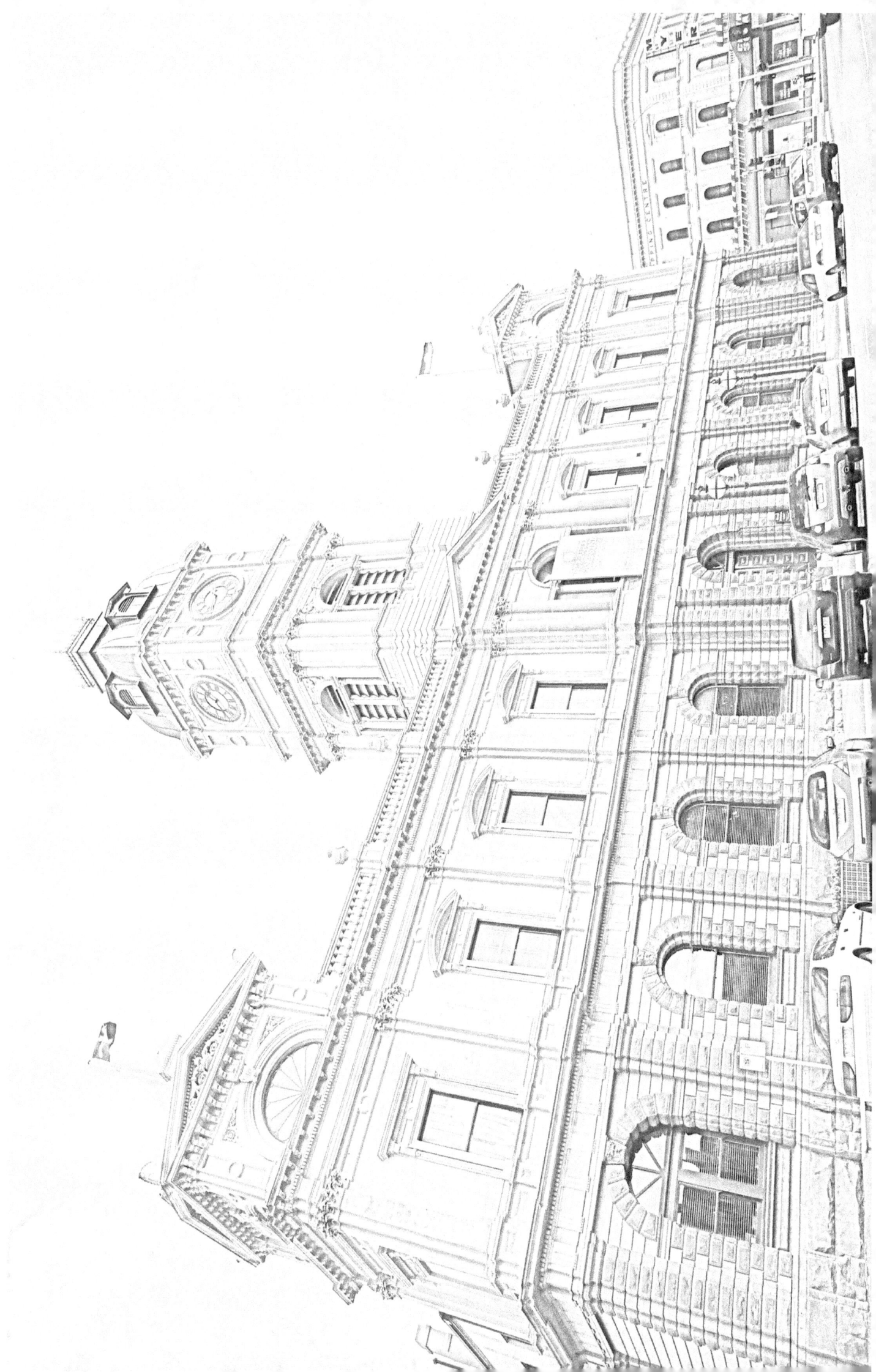

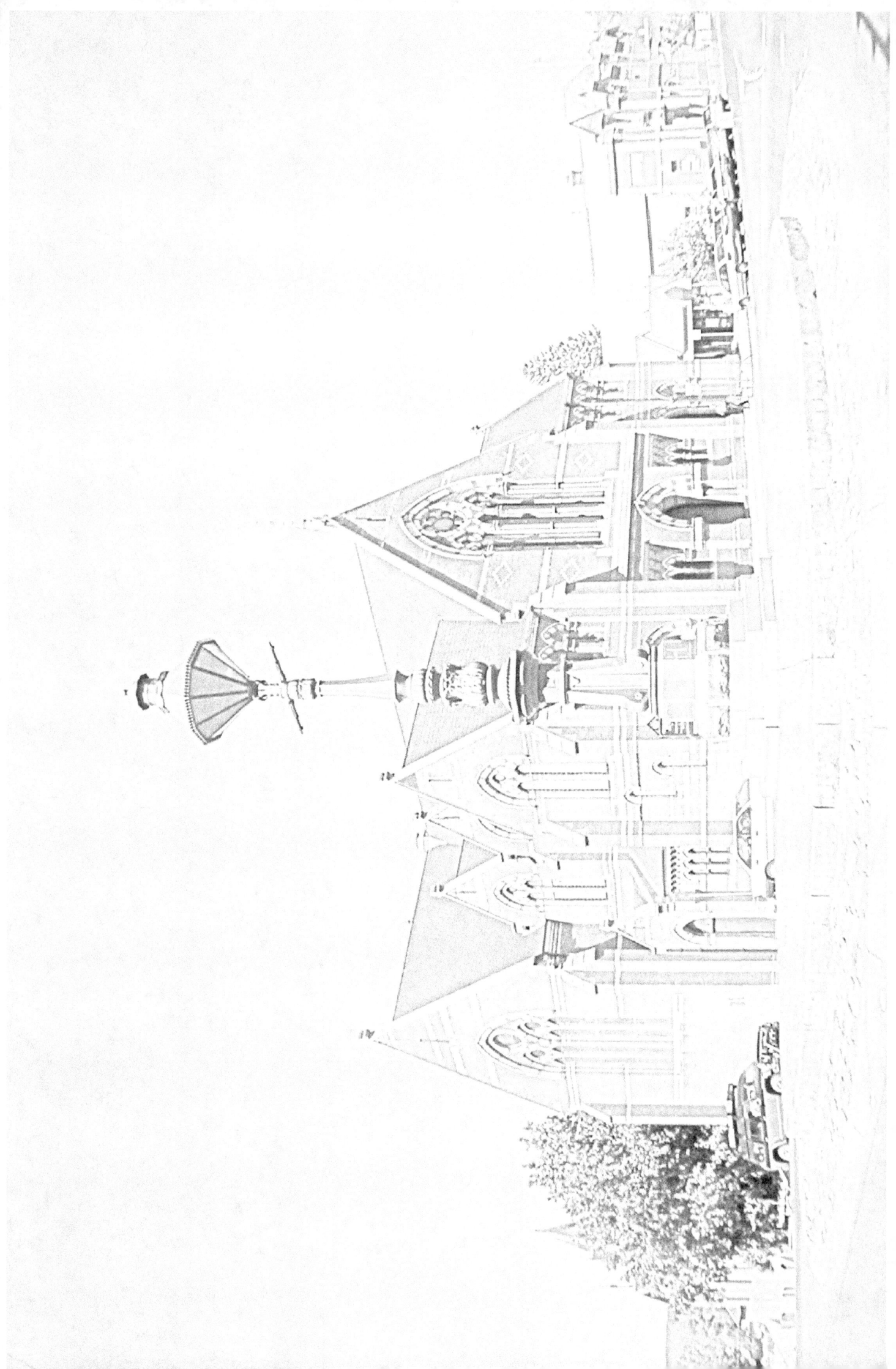

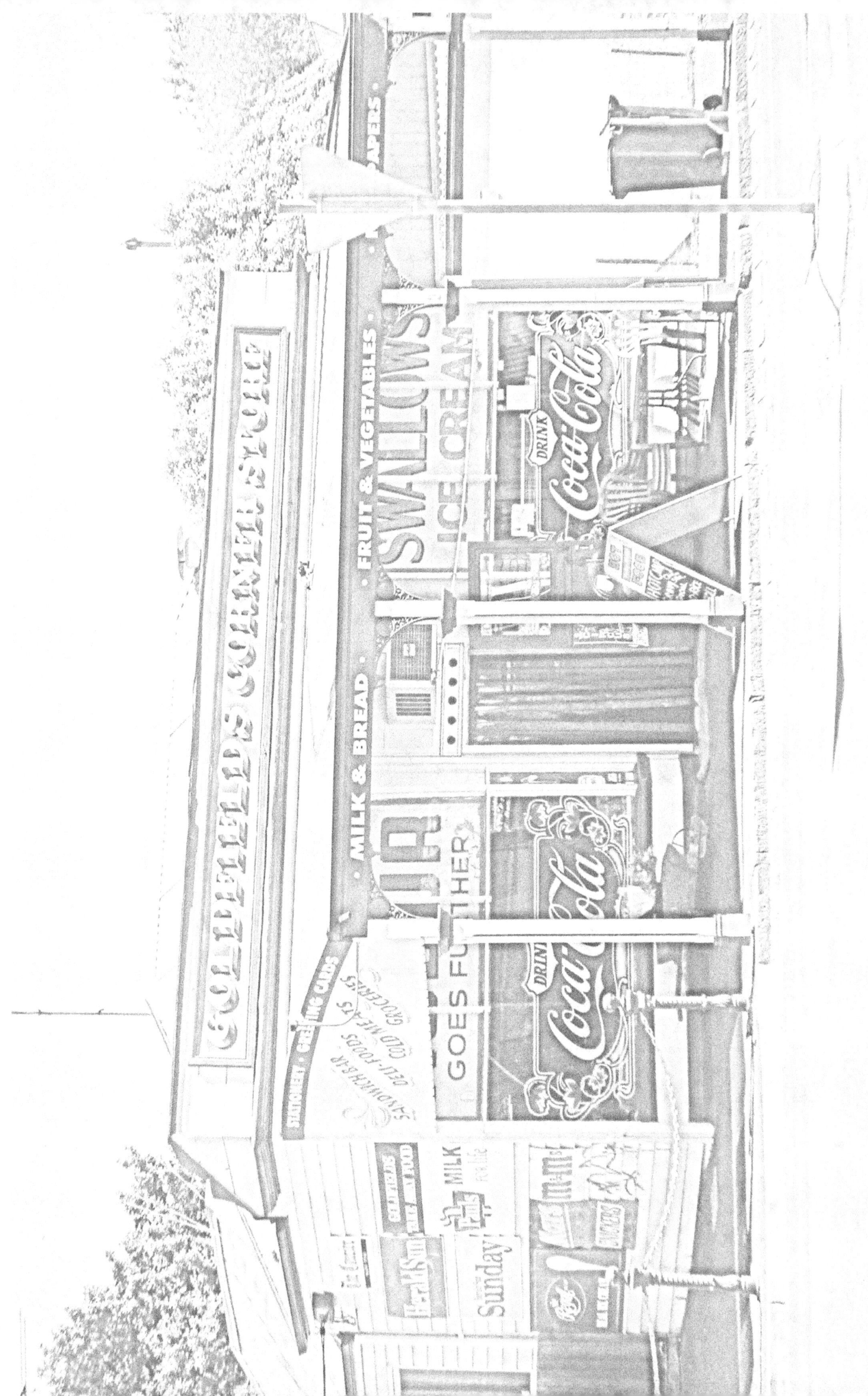

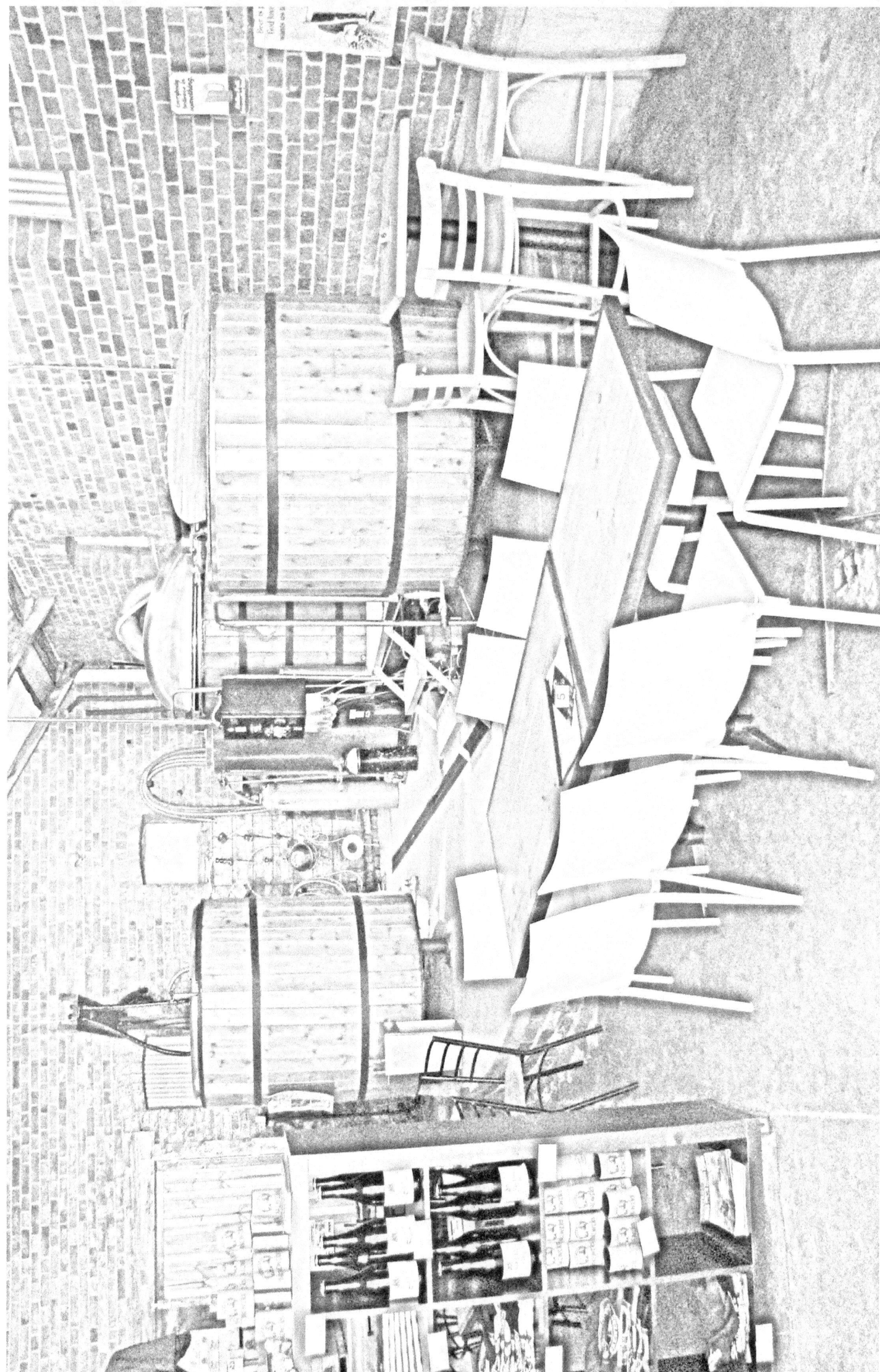

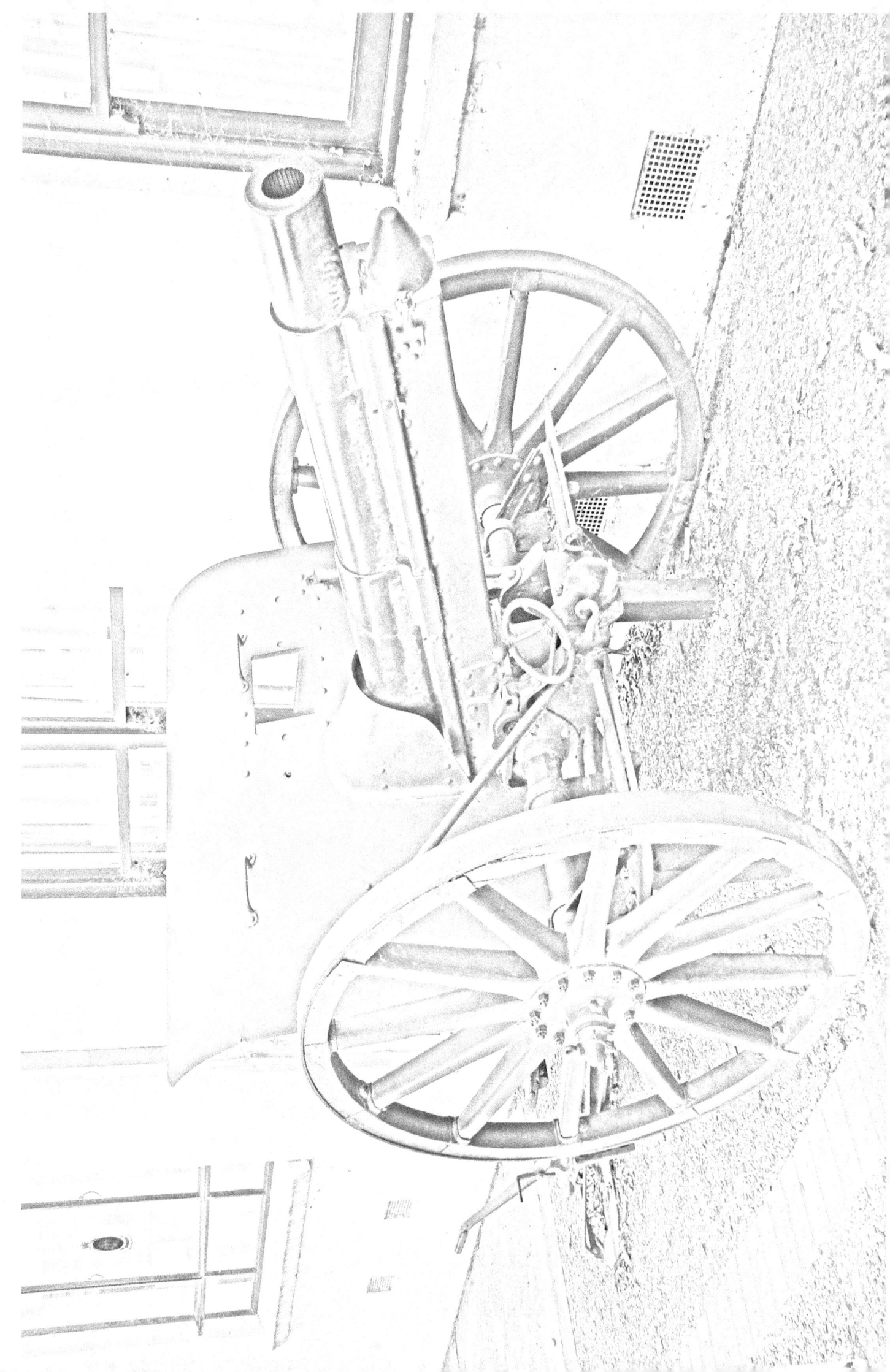

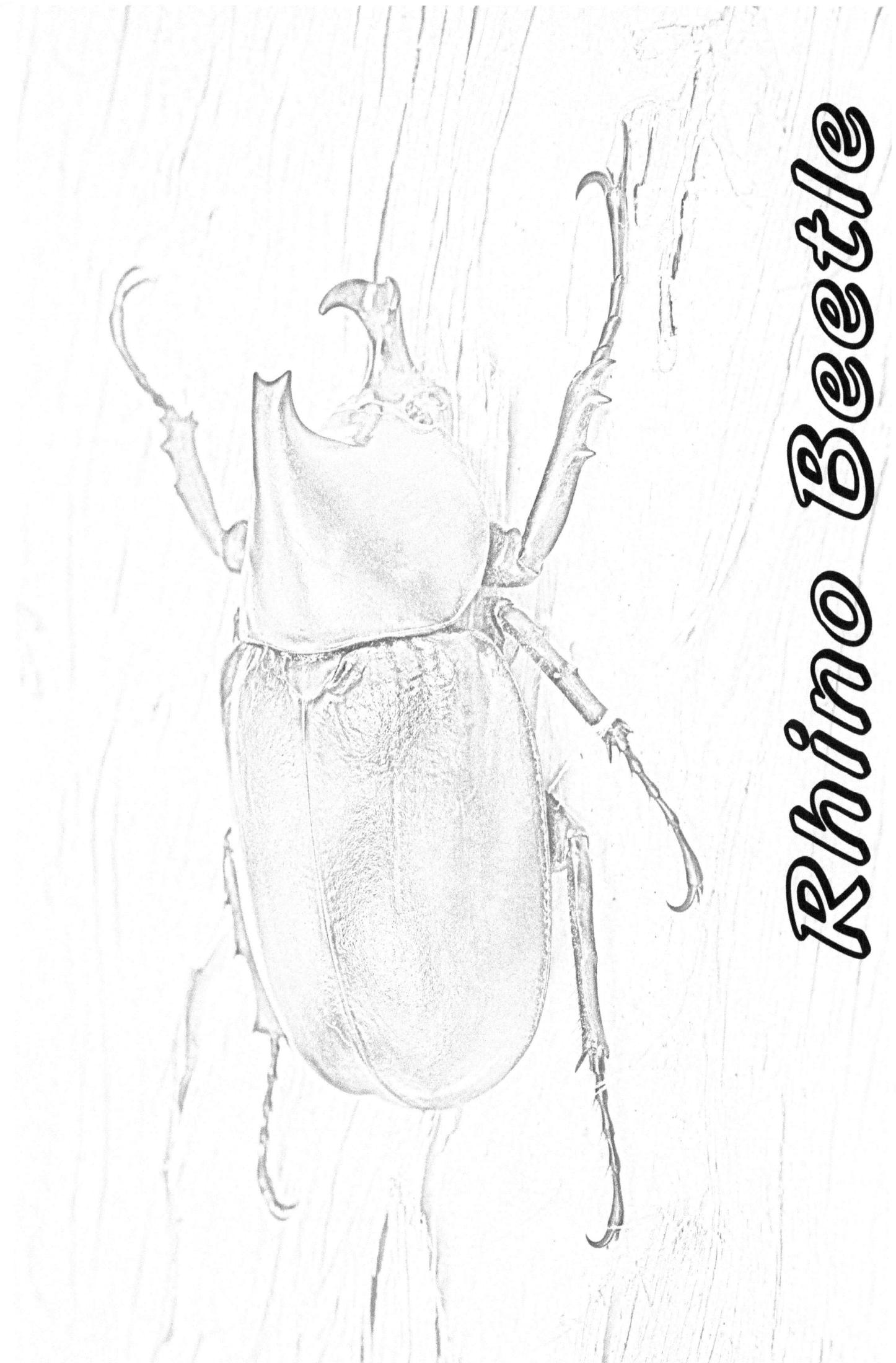

Rhino Beeetle

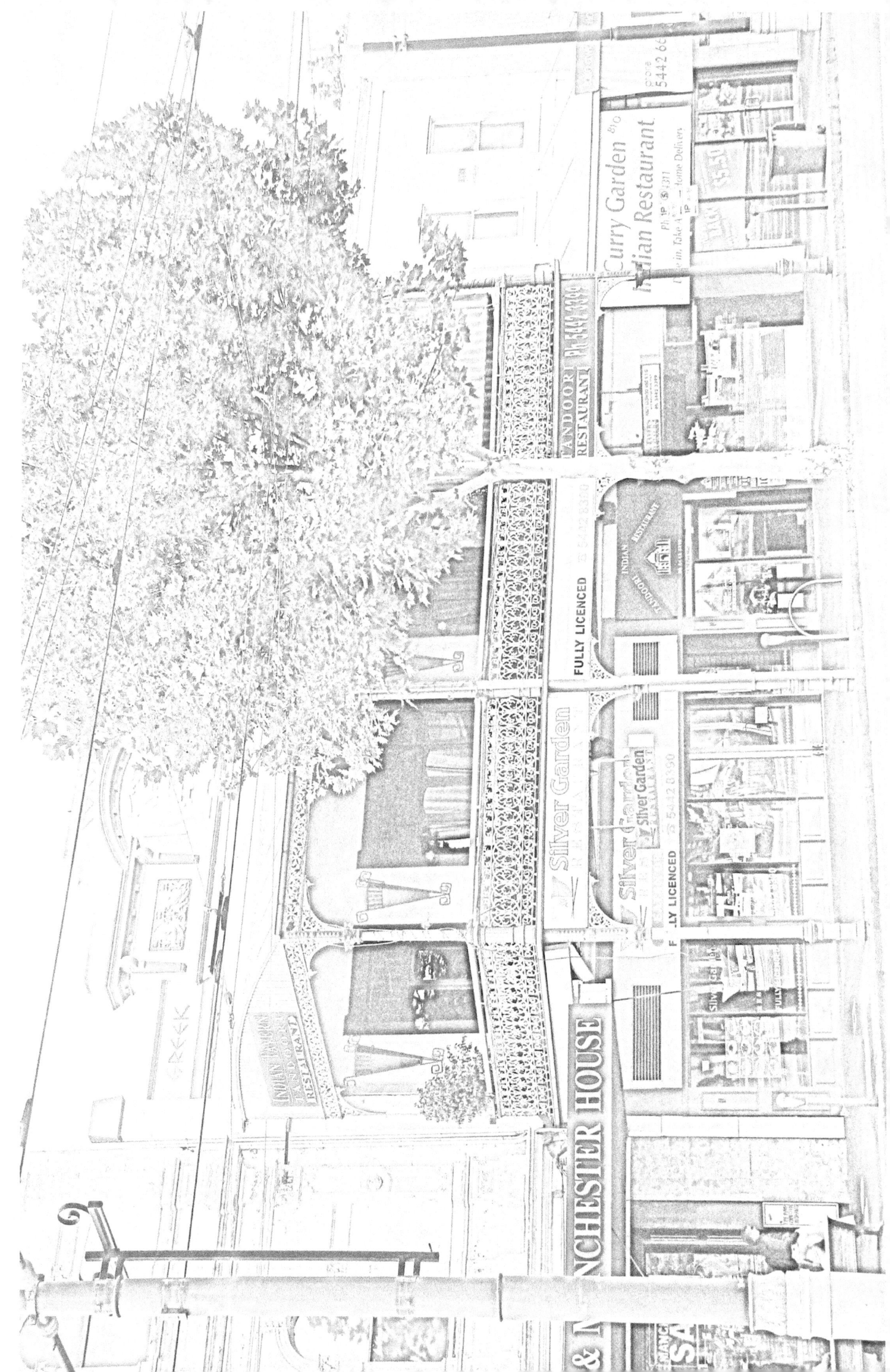

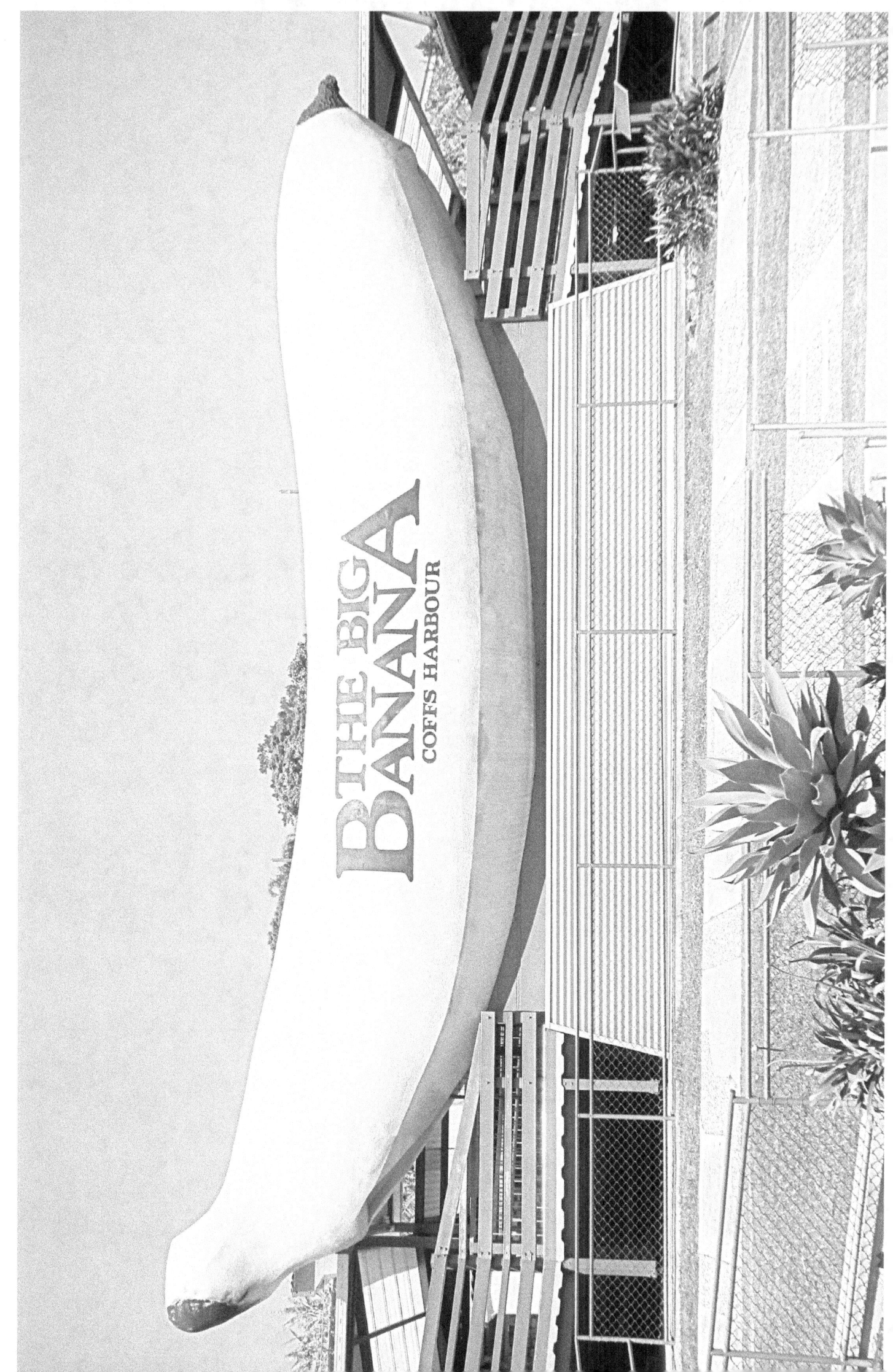

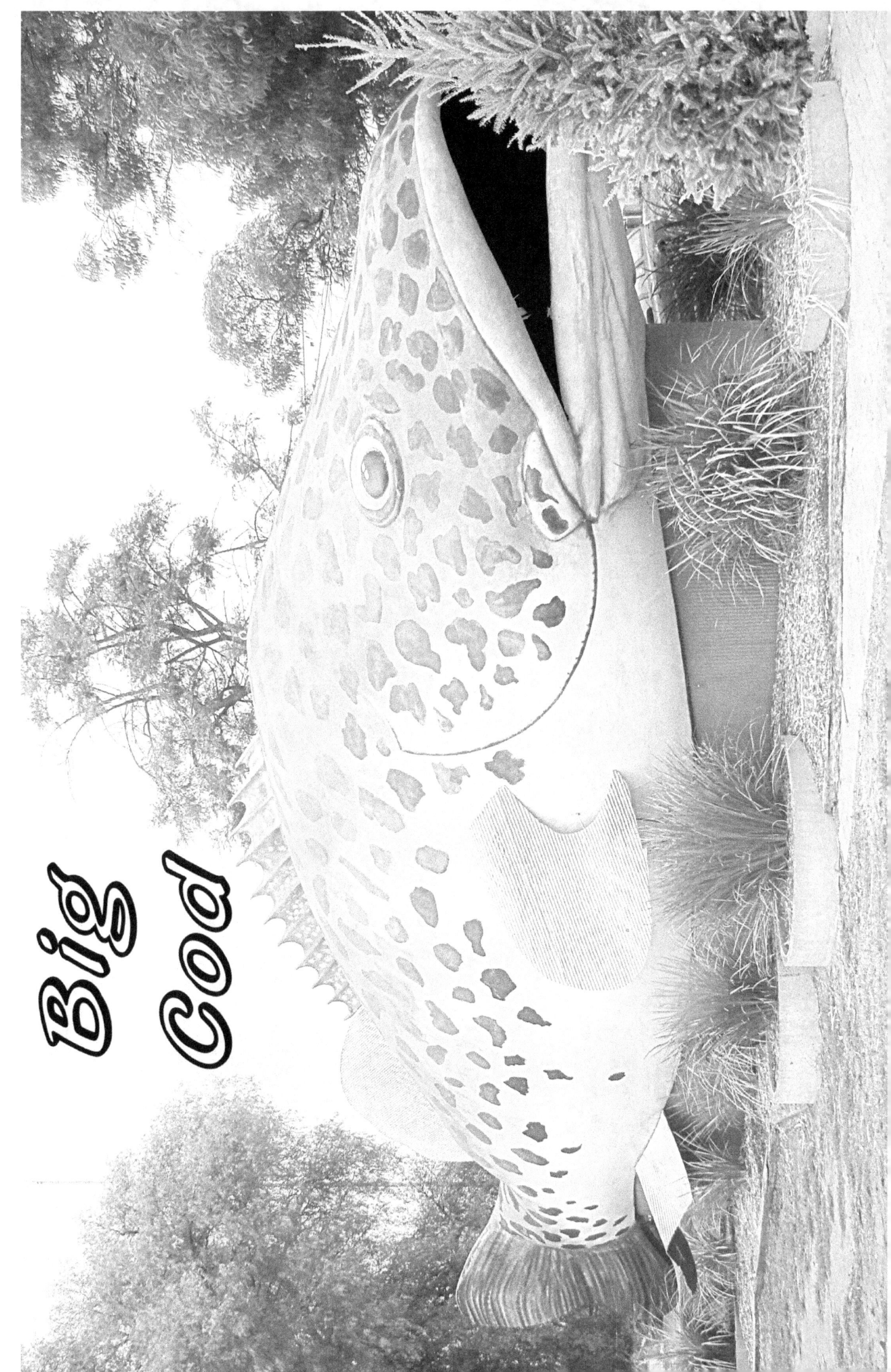

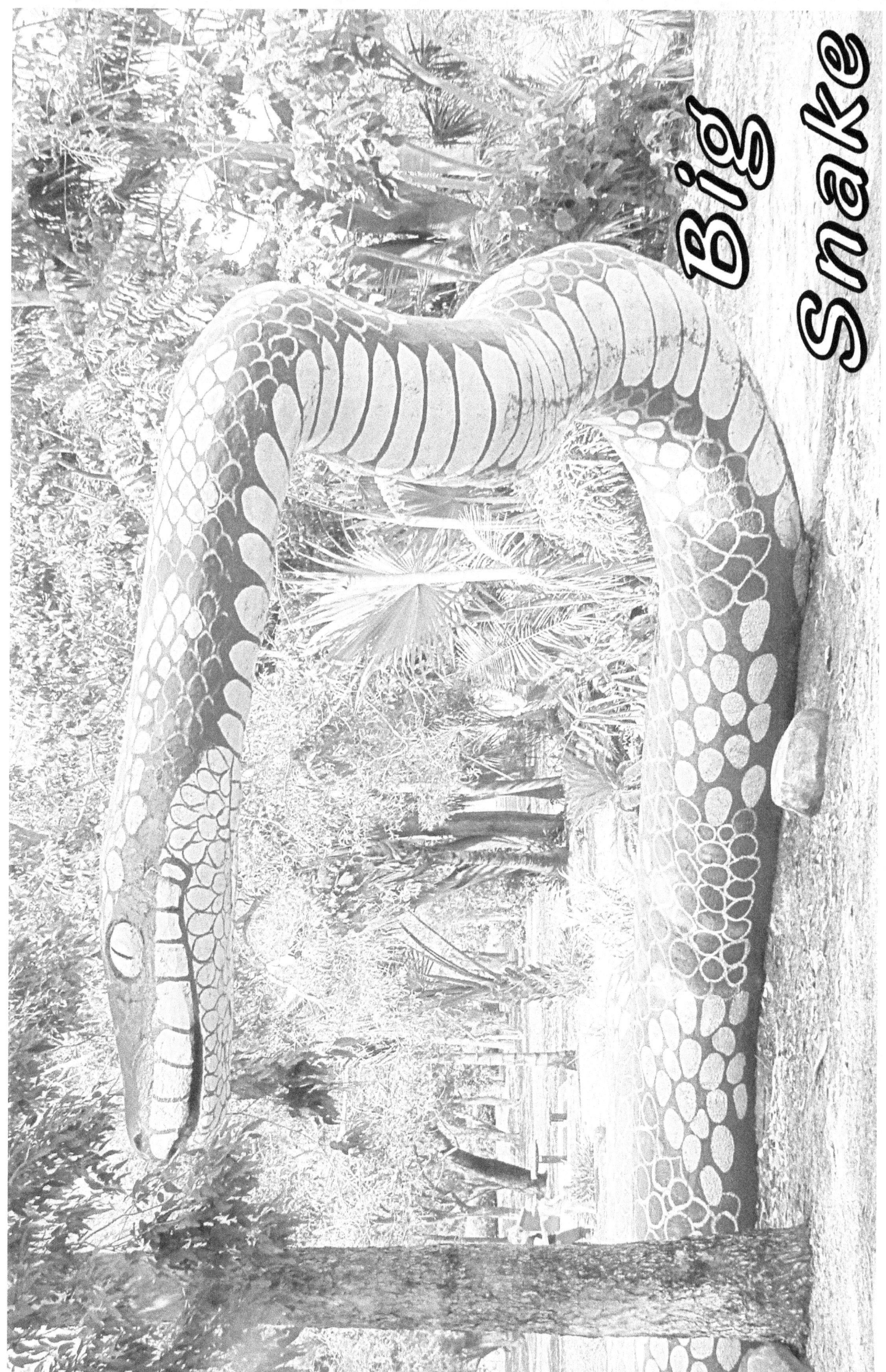

Big Snake

River Boat

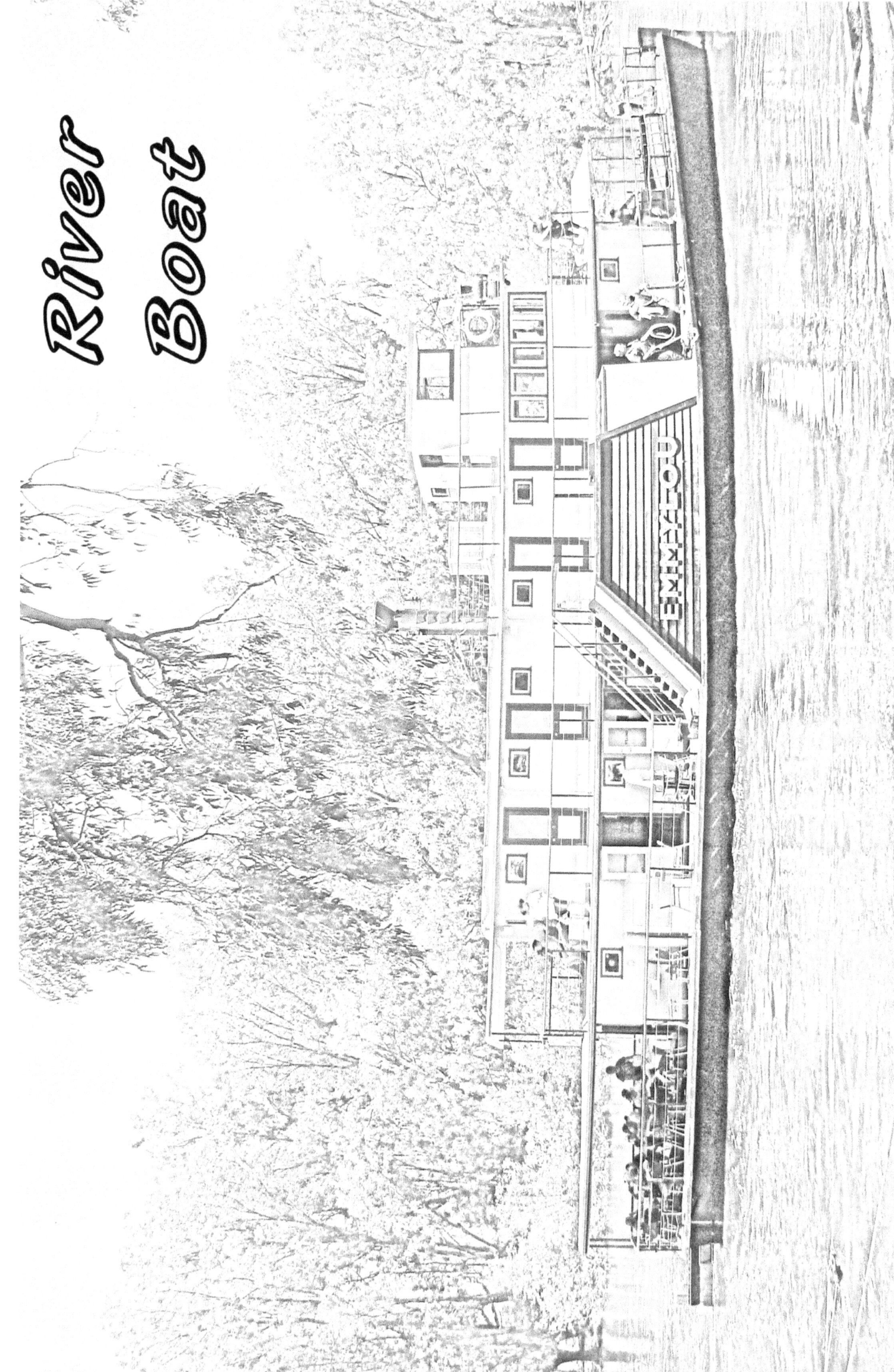

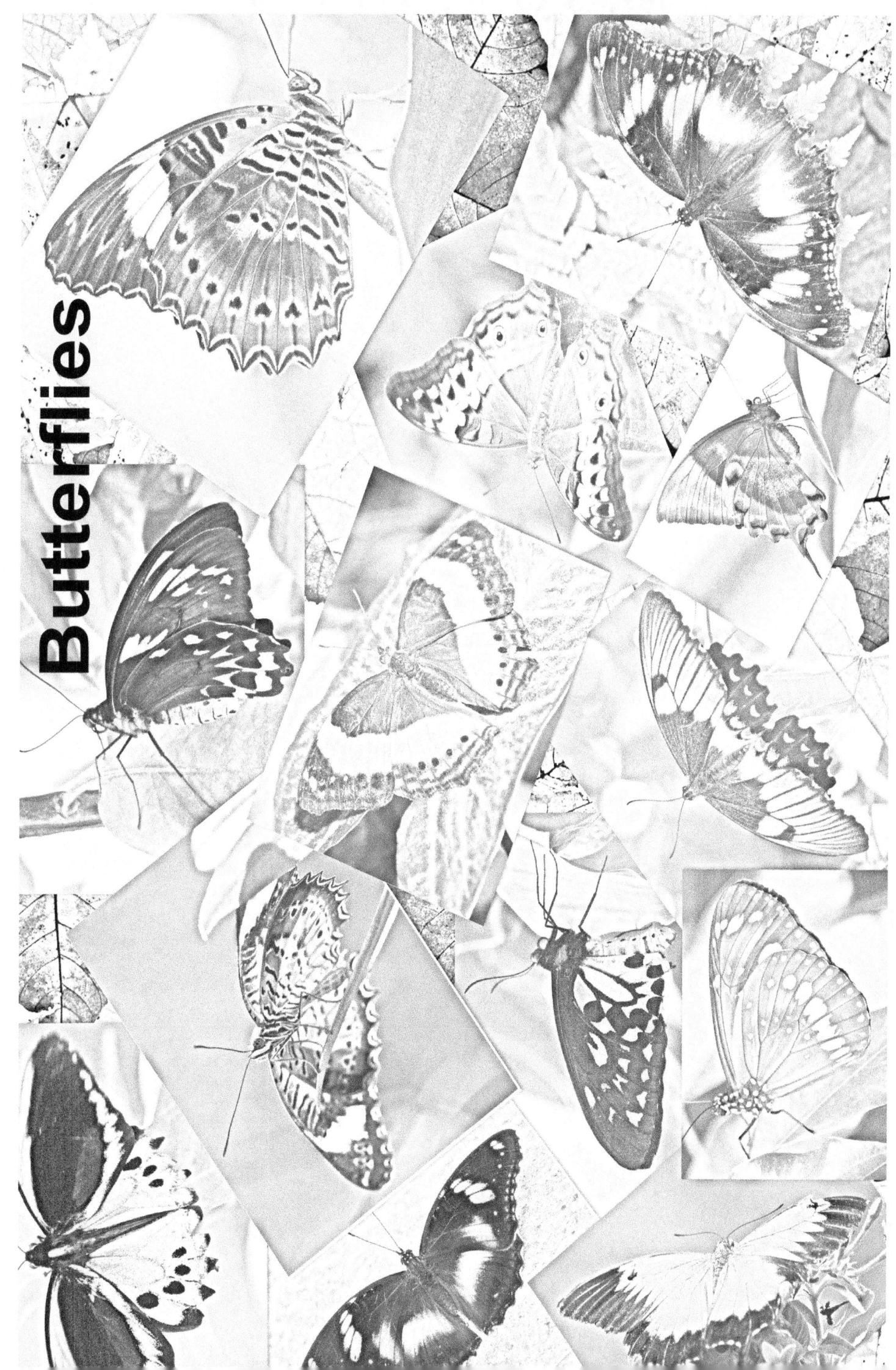

Butterflies

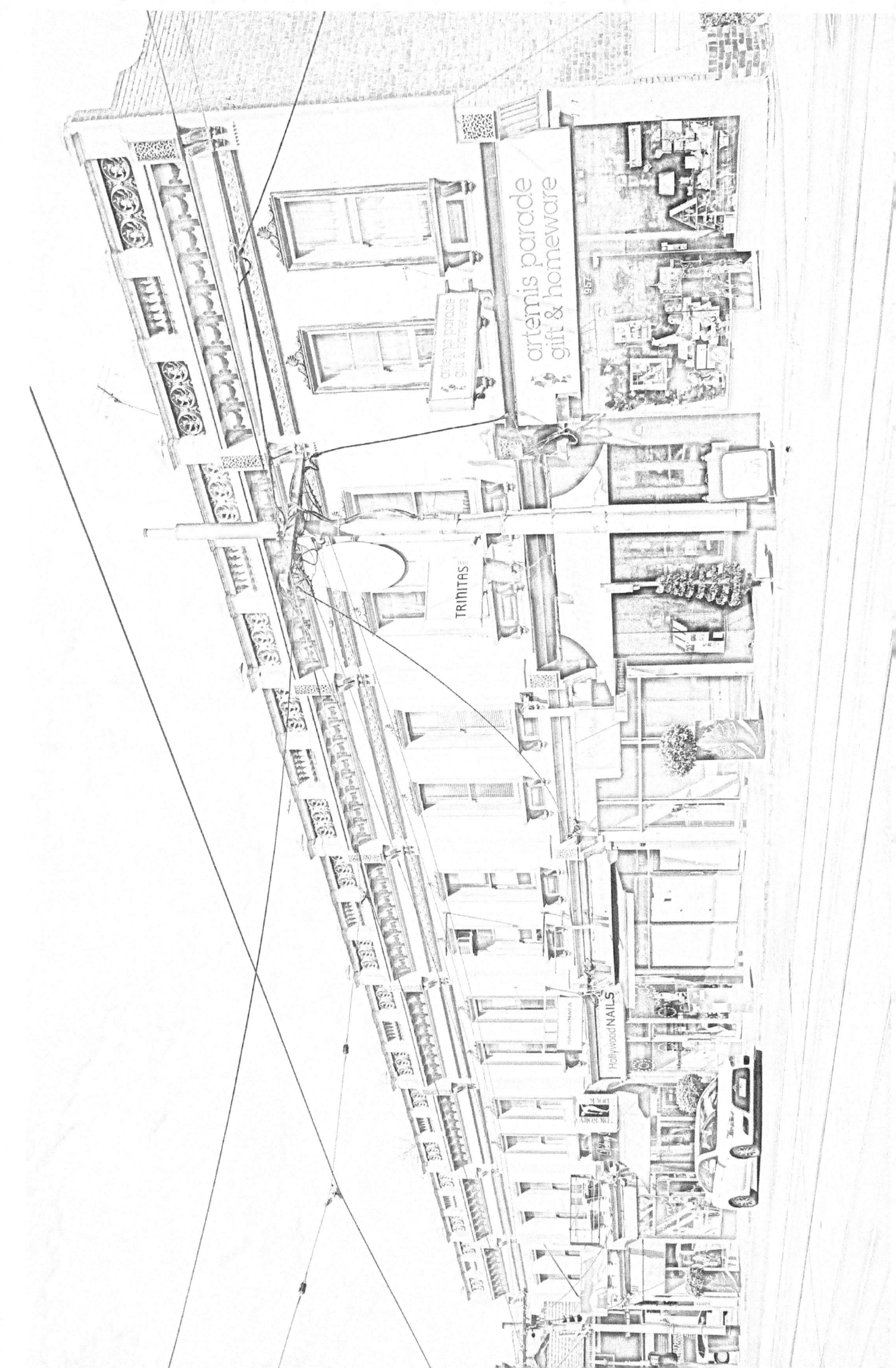

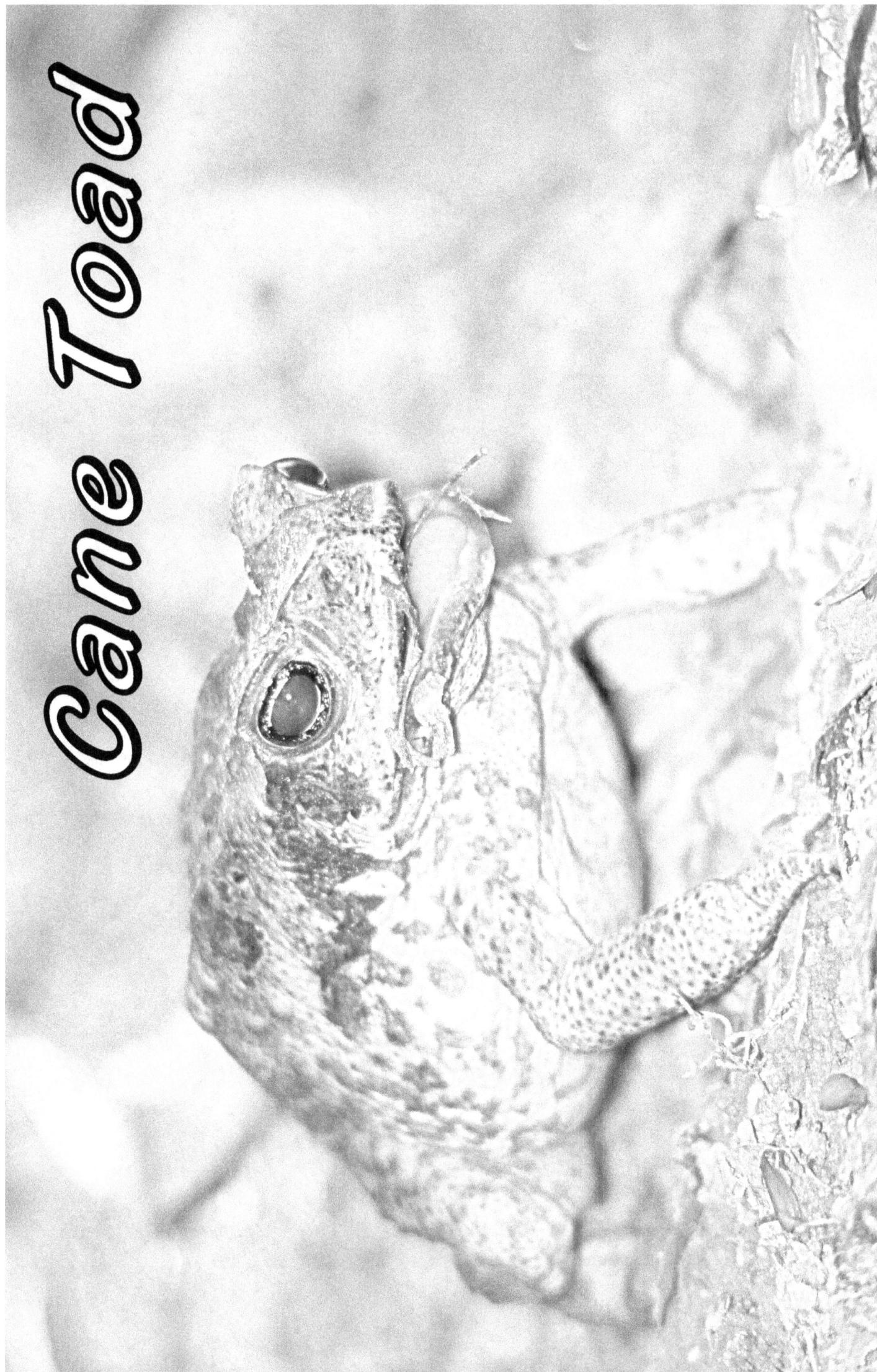

Cane Toad

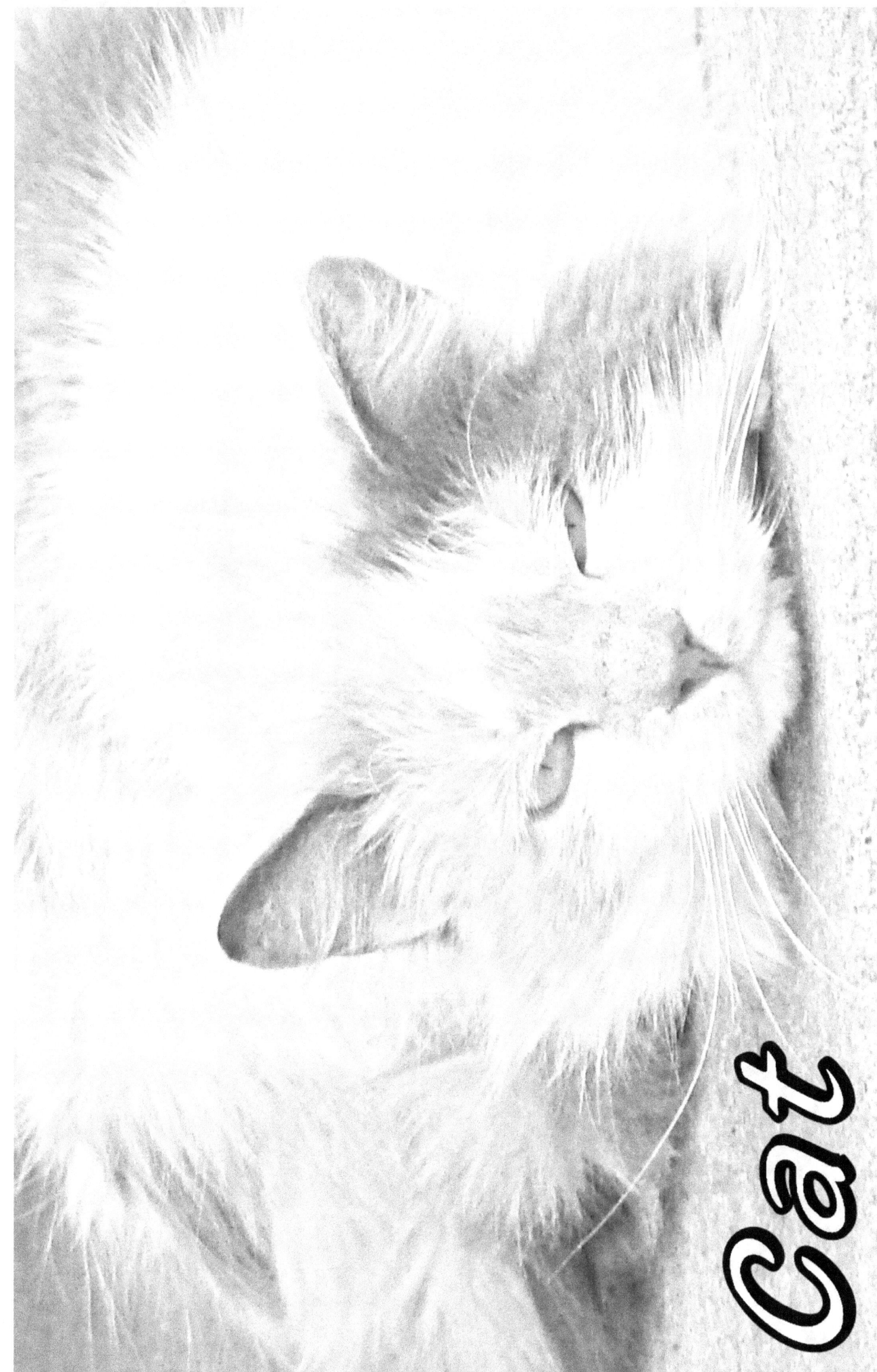

Cat

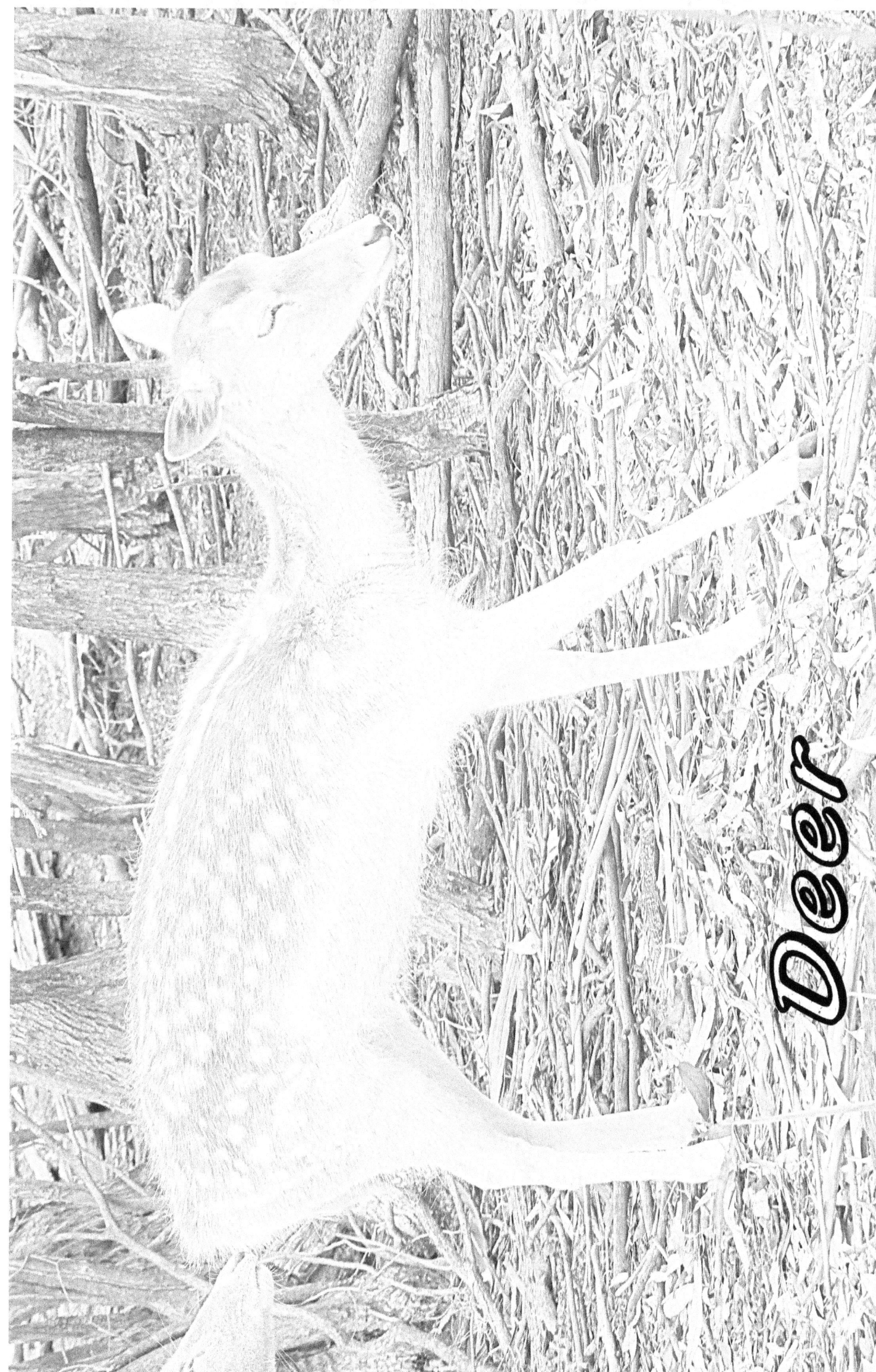

Deer

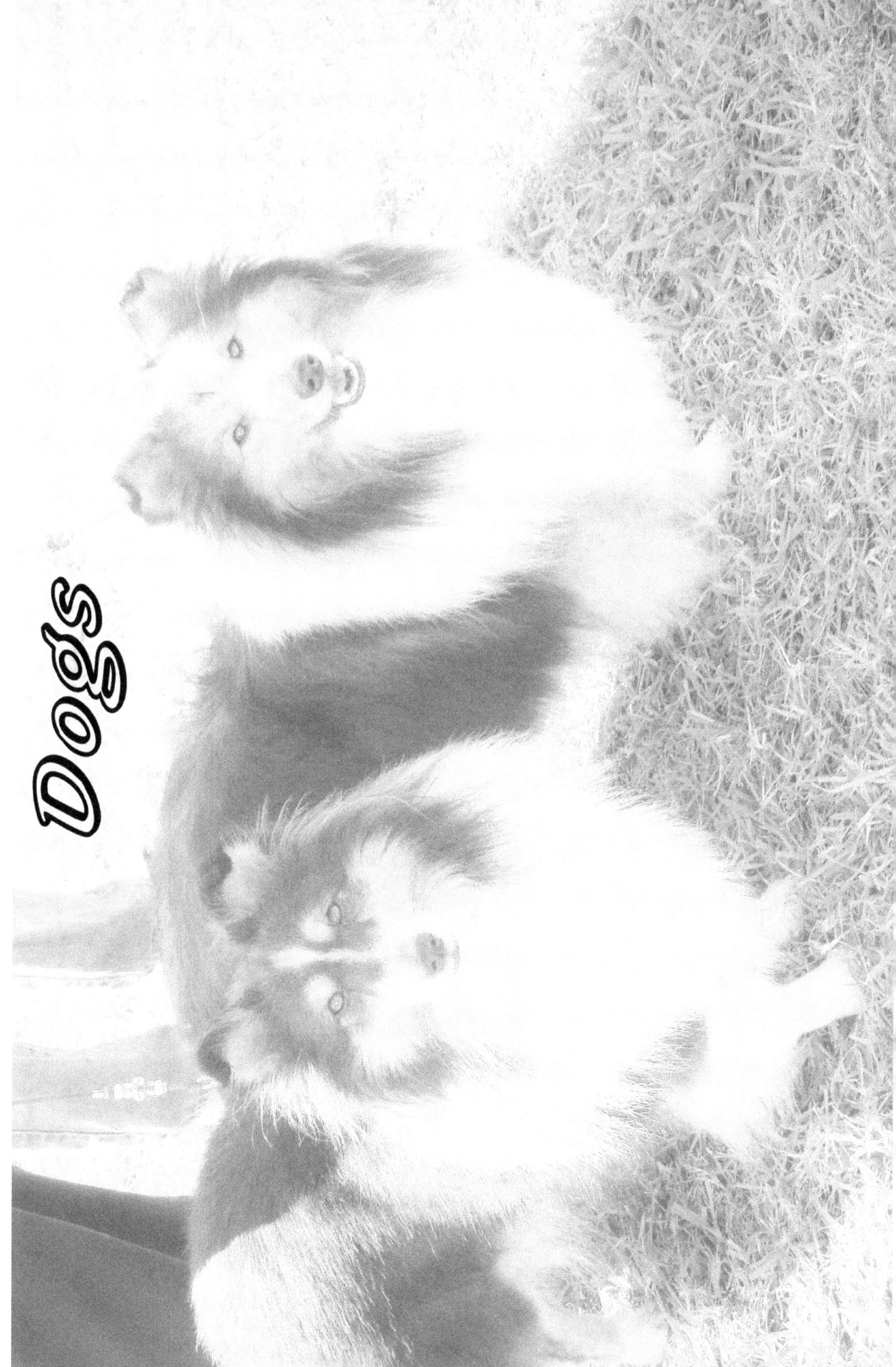

Dogs

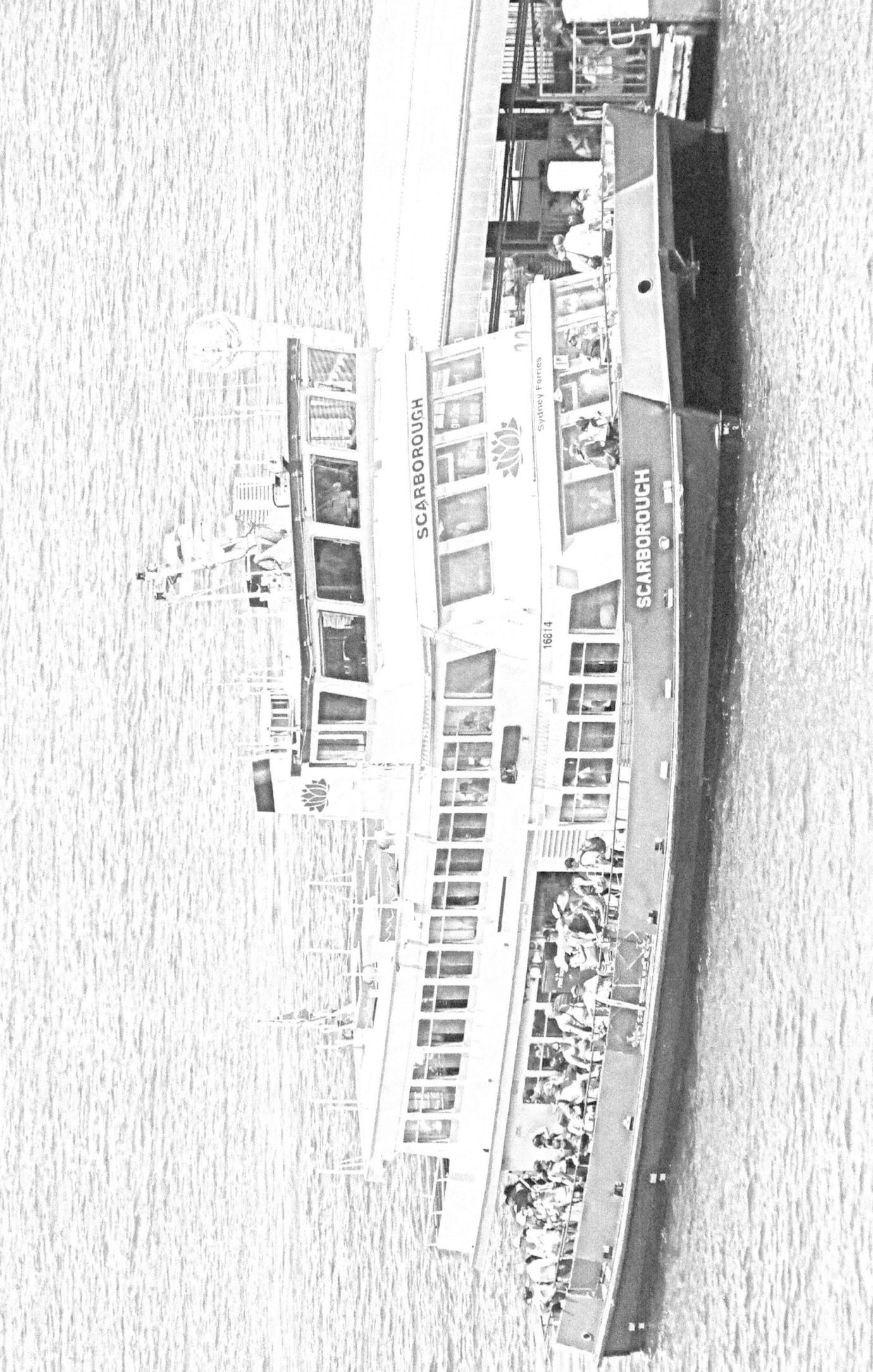

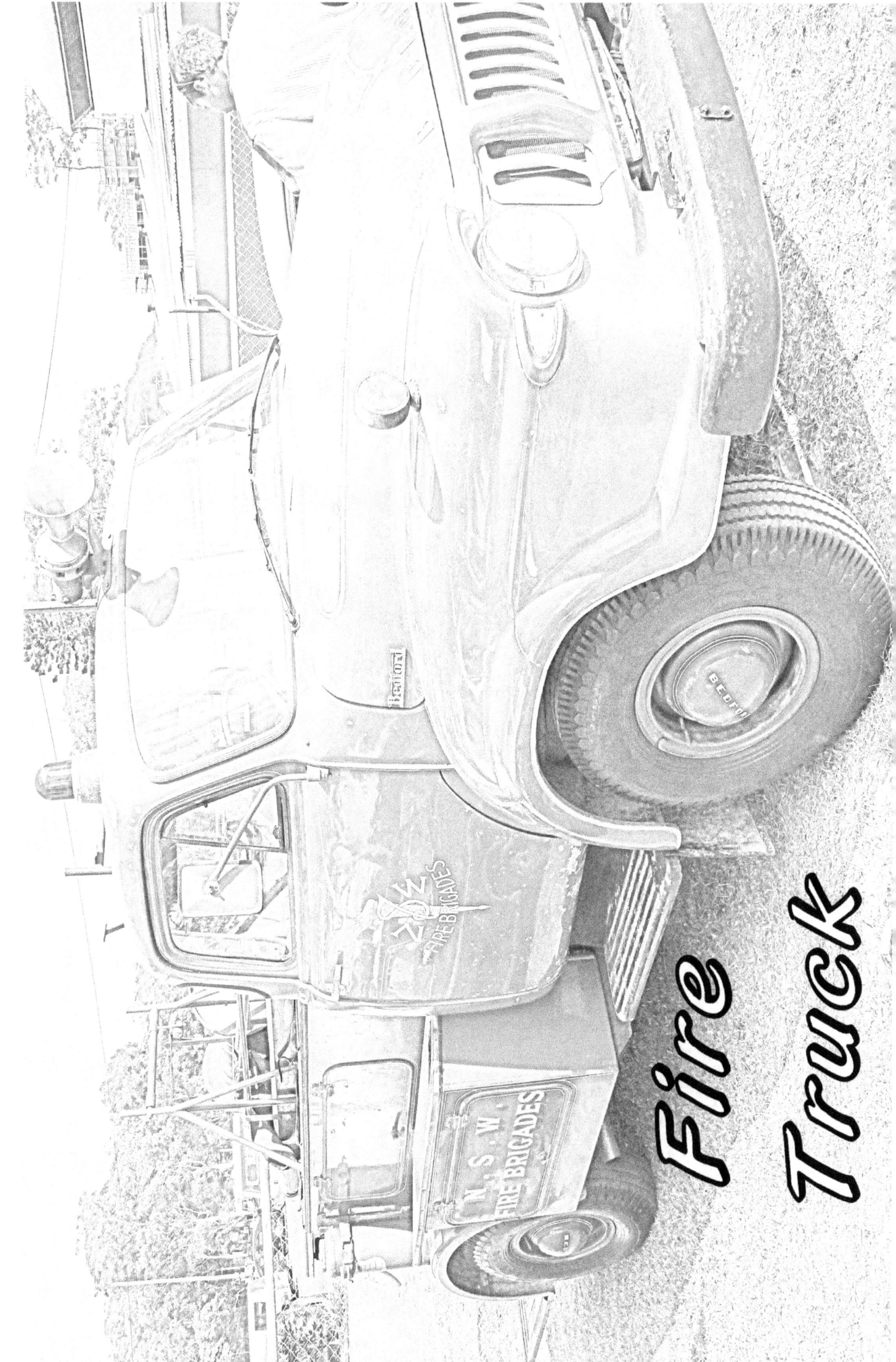

Fire Truck

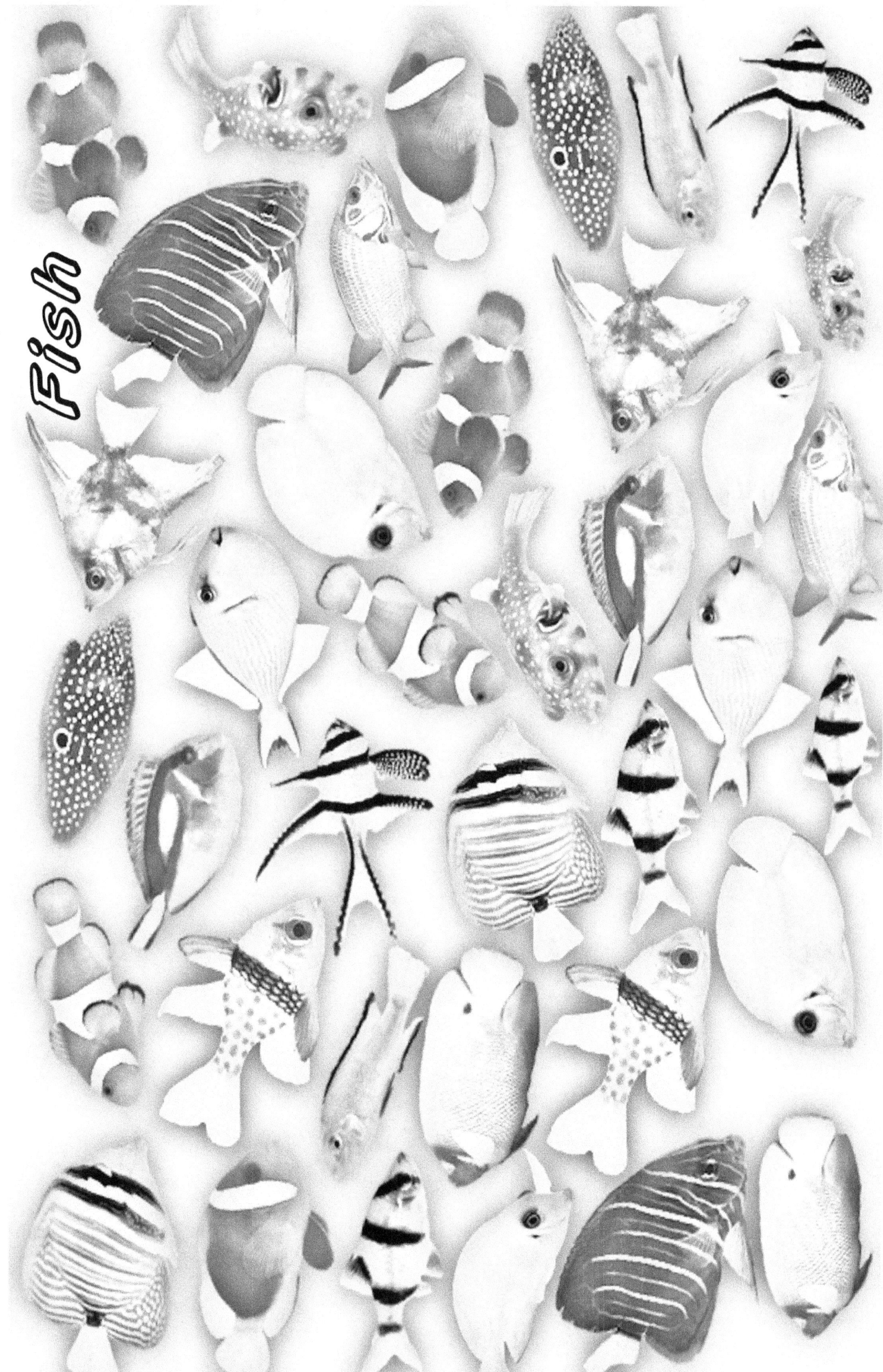

Fish

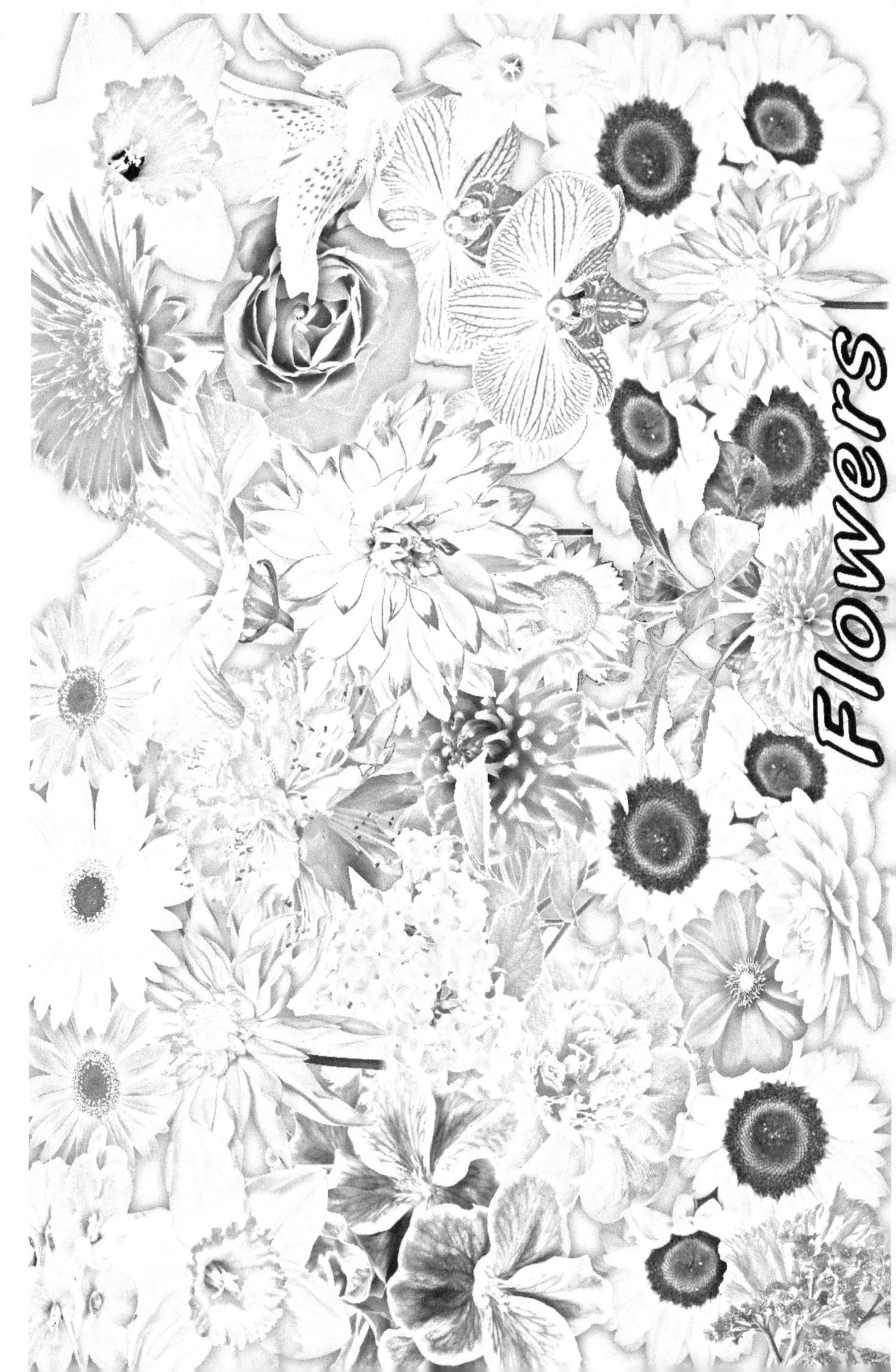

Flowers

Goanna

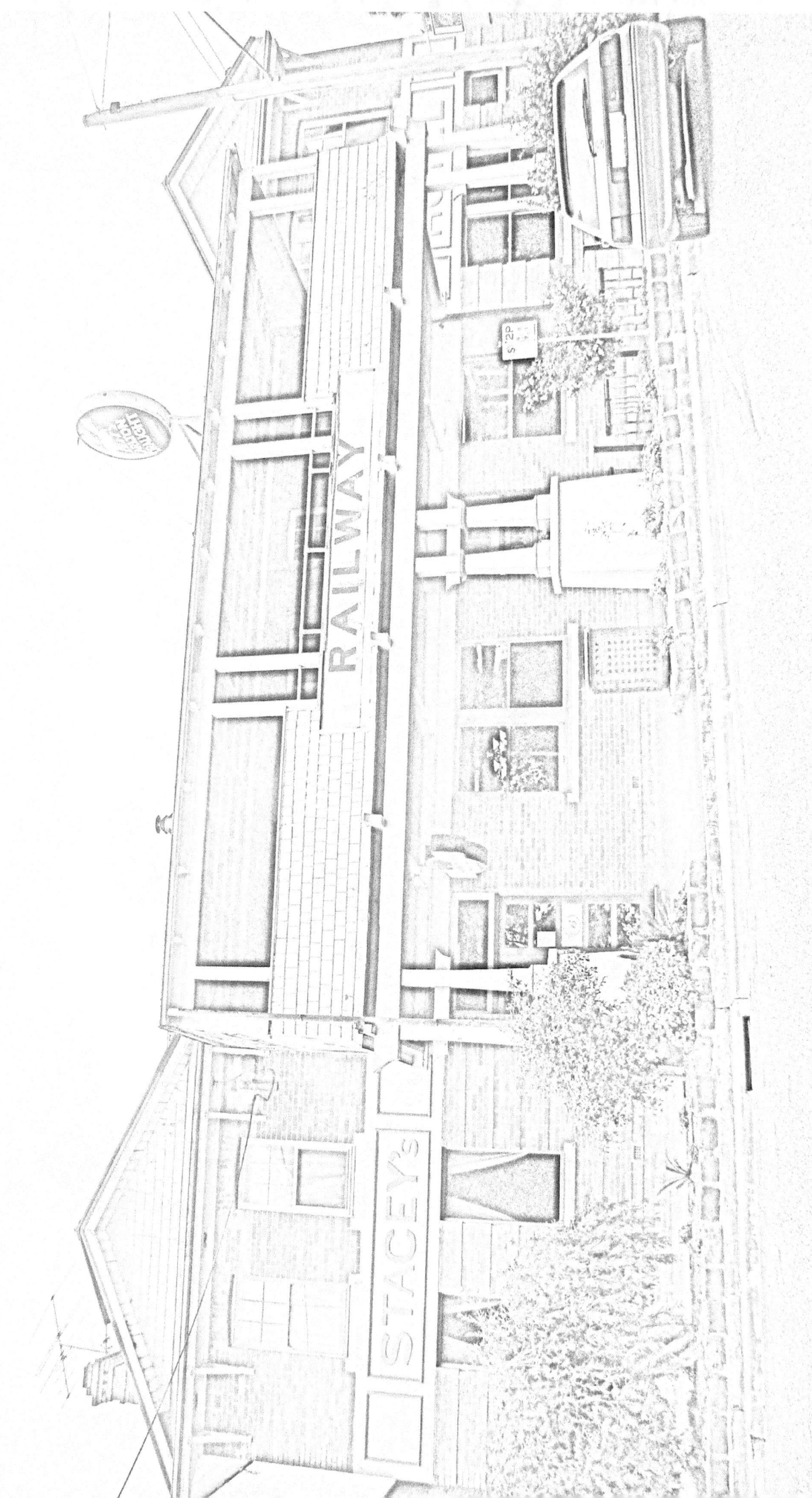

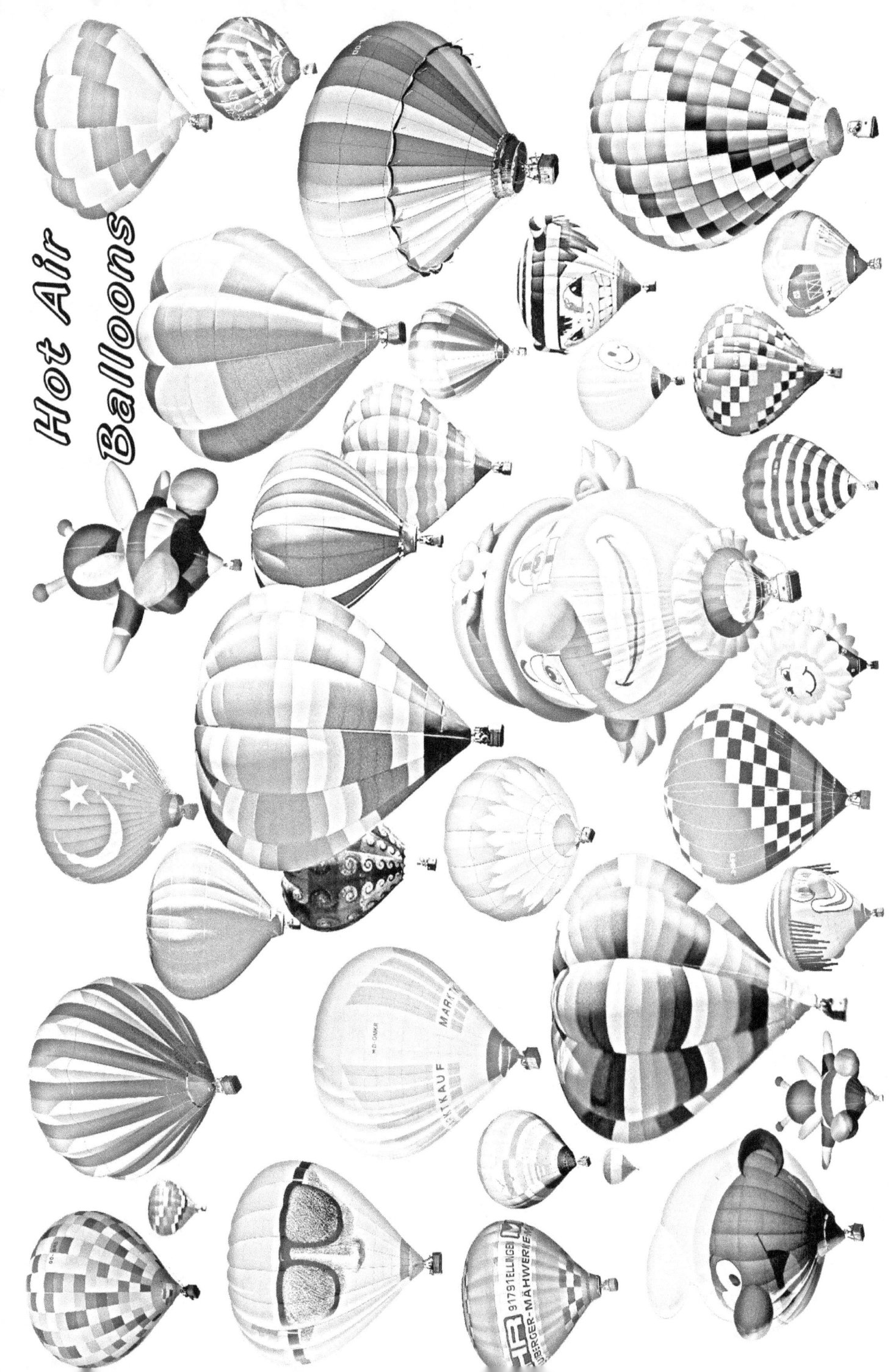

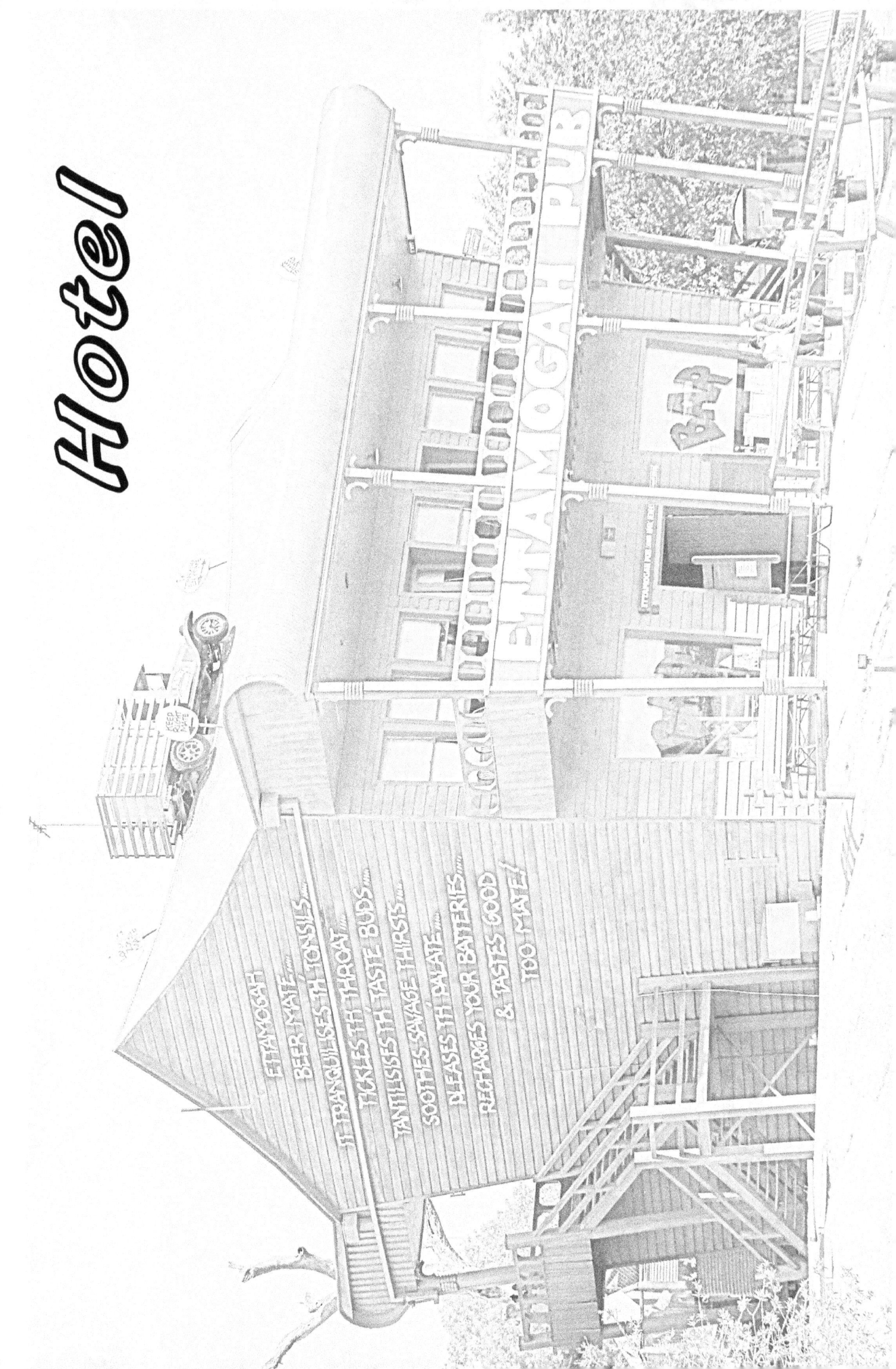

Hotel

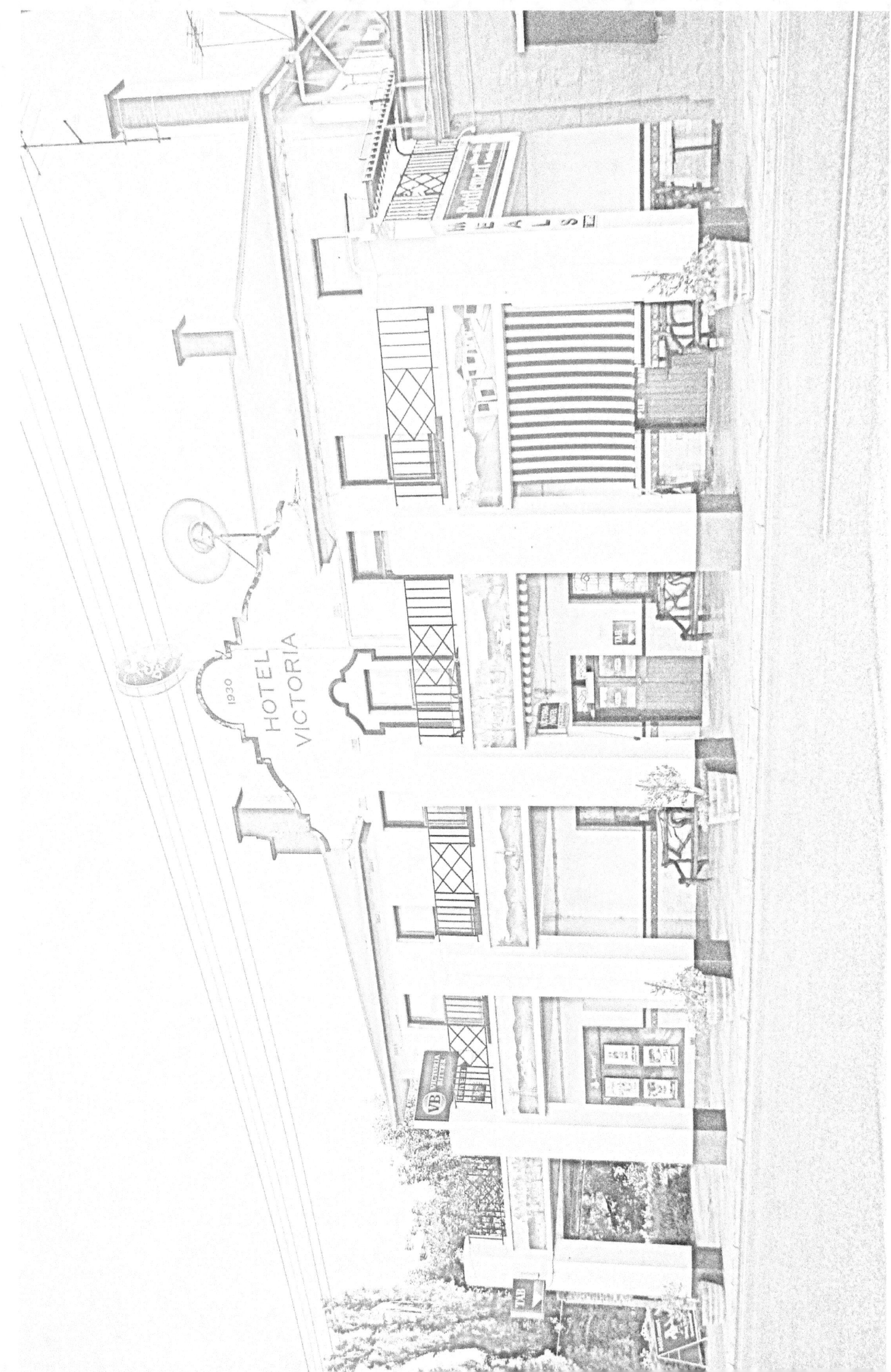

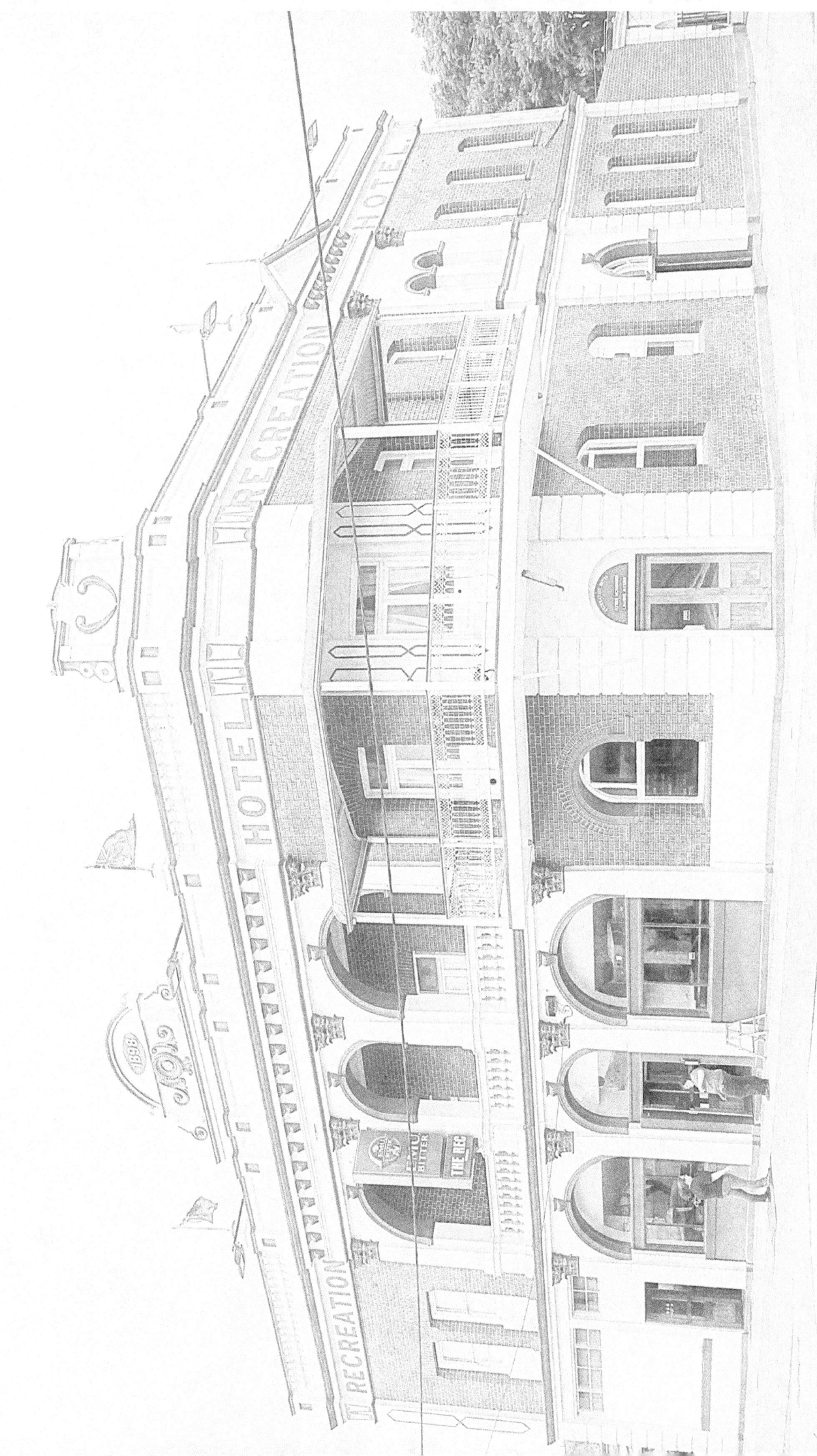

Zebra

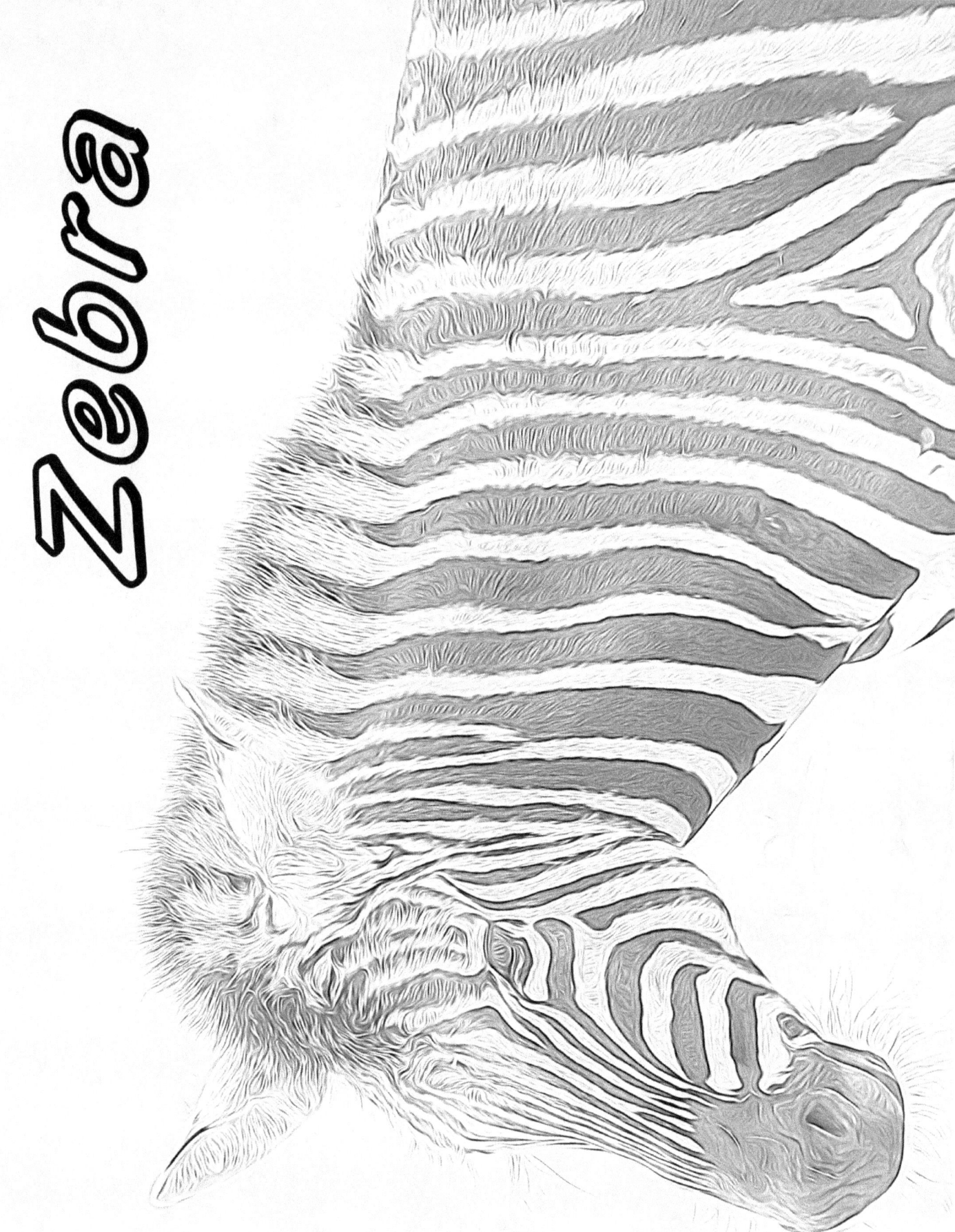

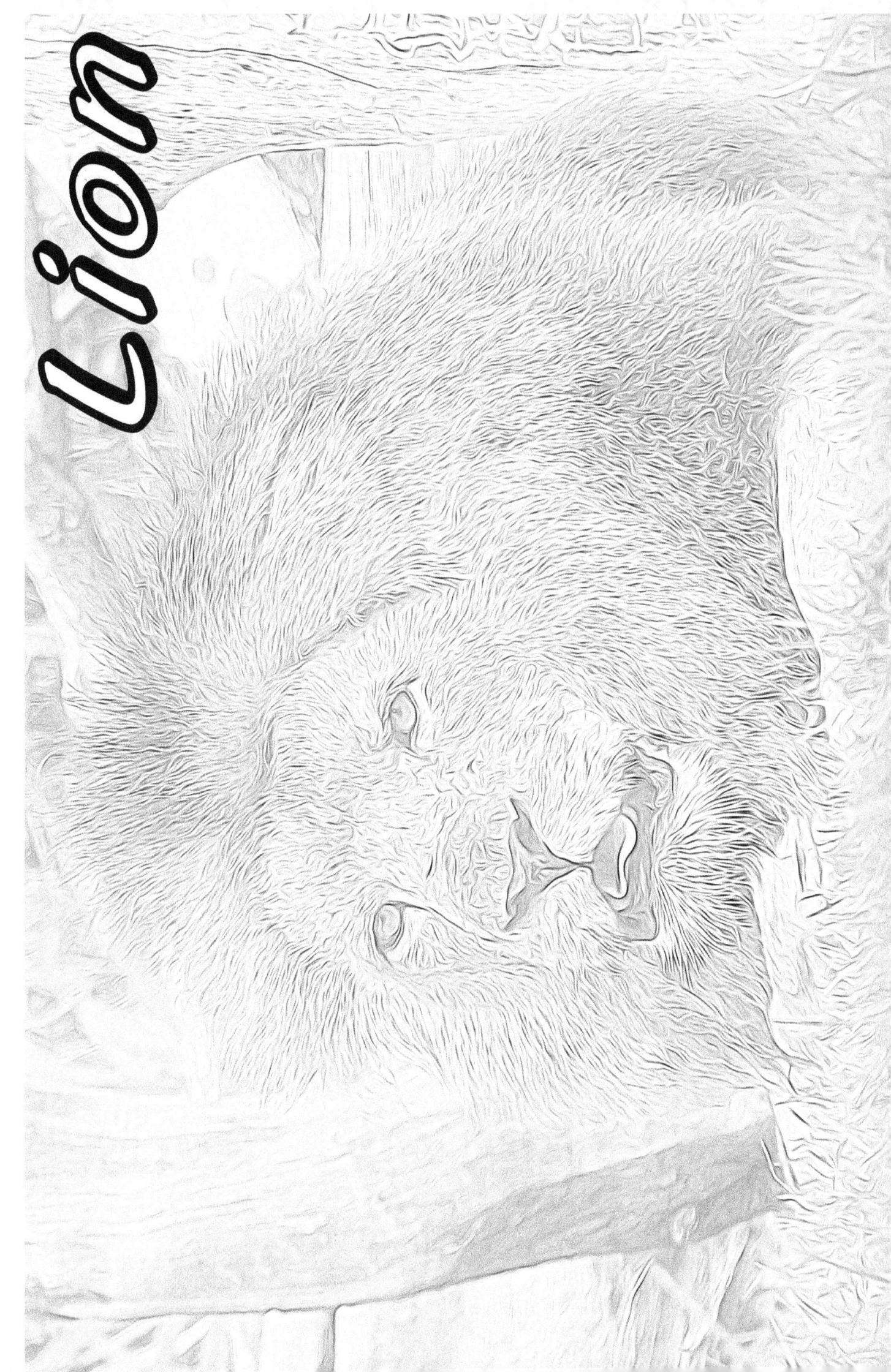

Lion

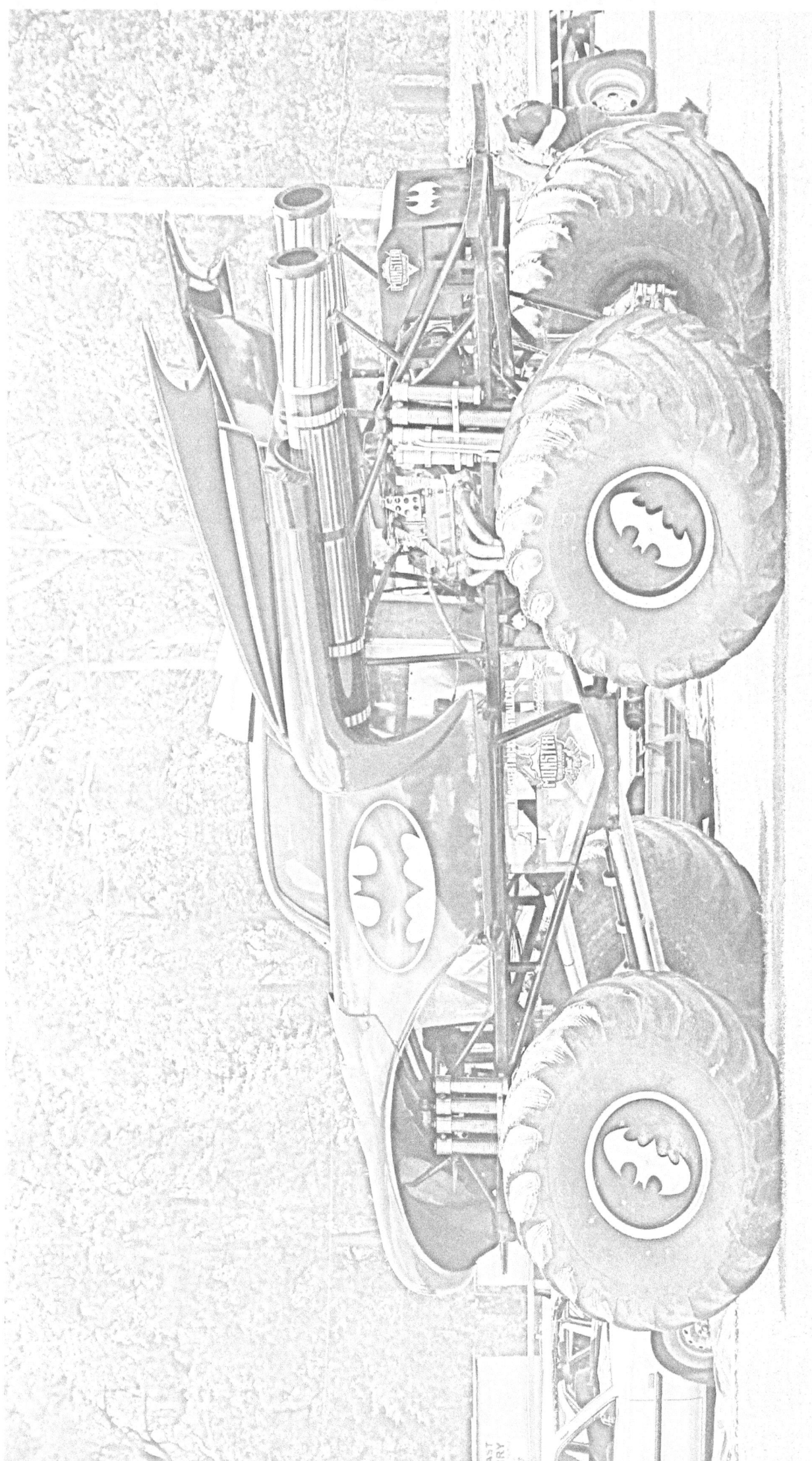

Monster Truck

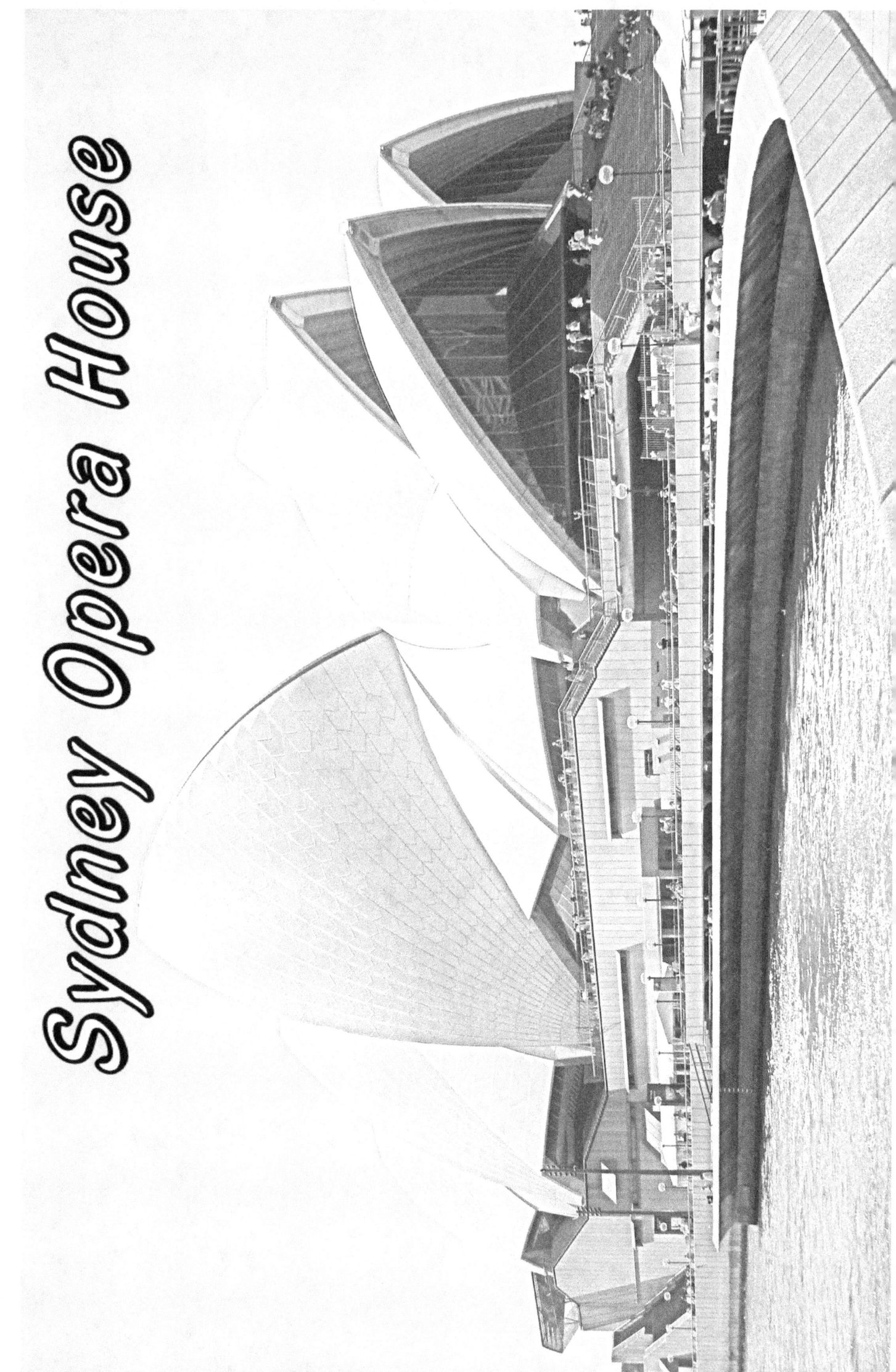

Sydney Opera House

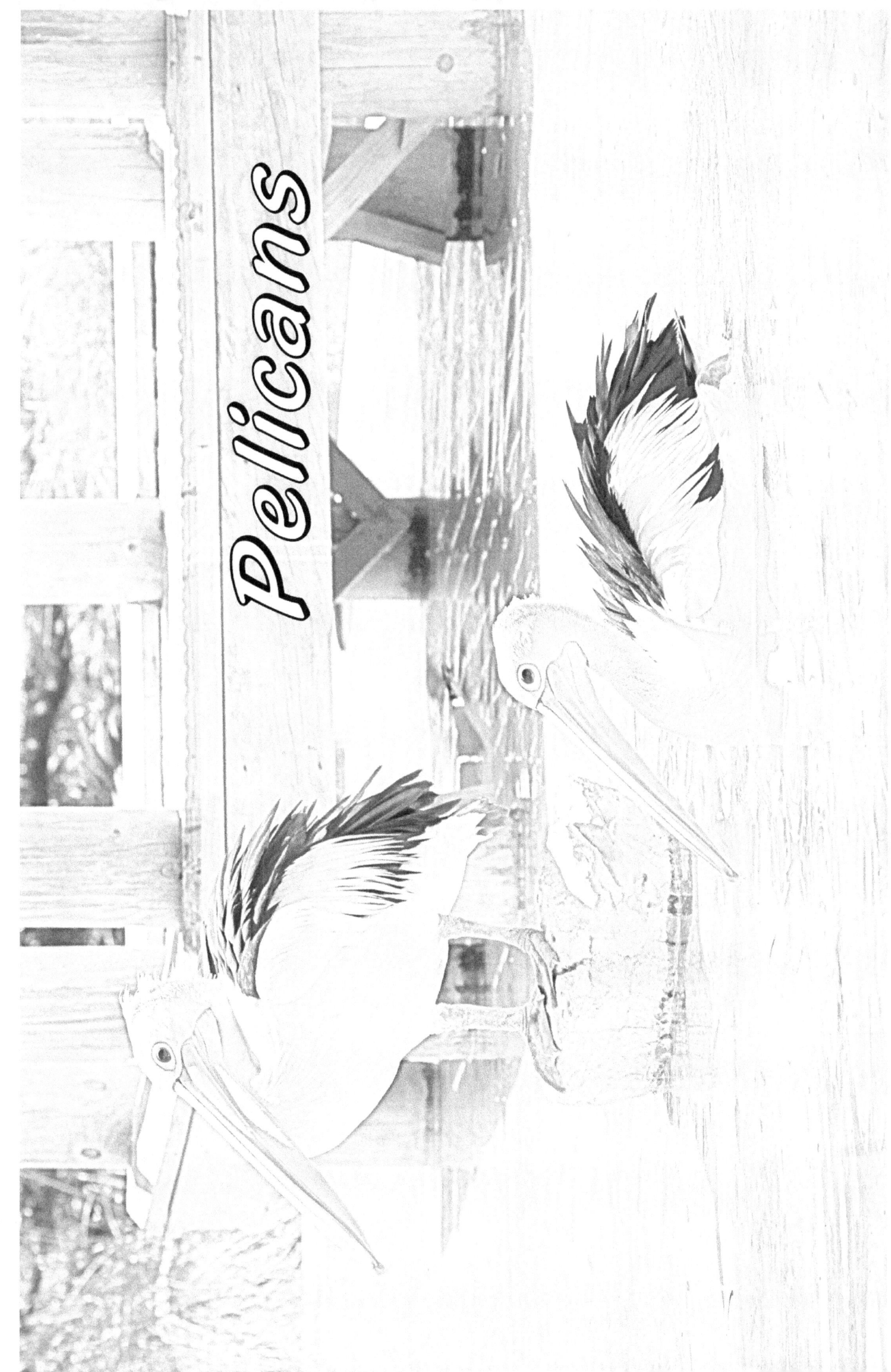

Pelicans

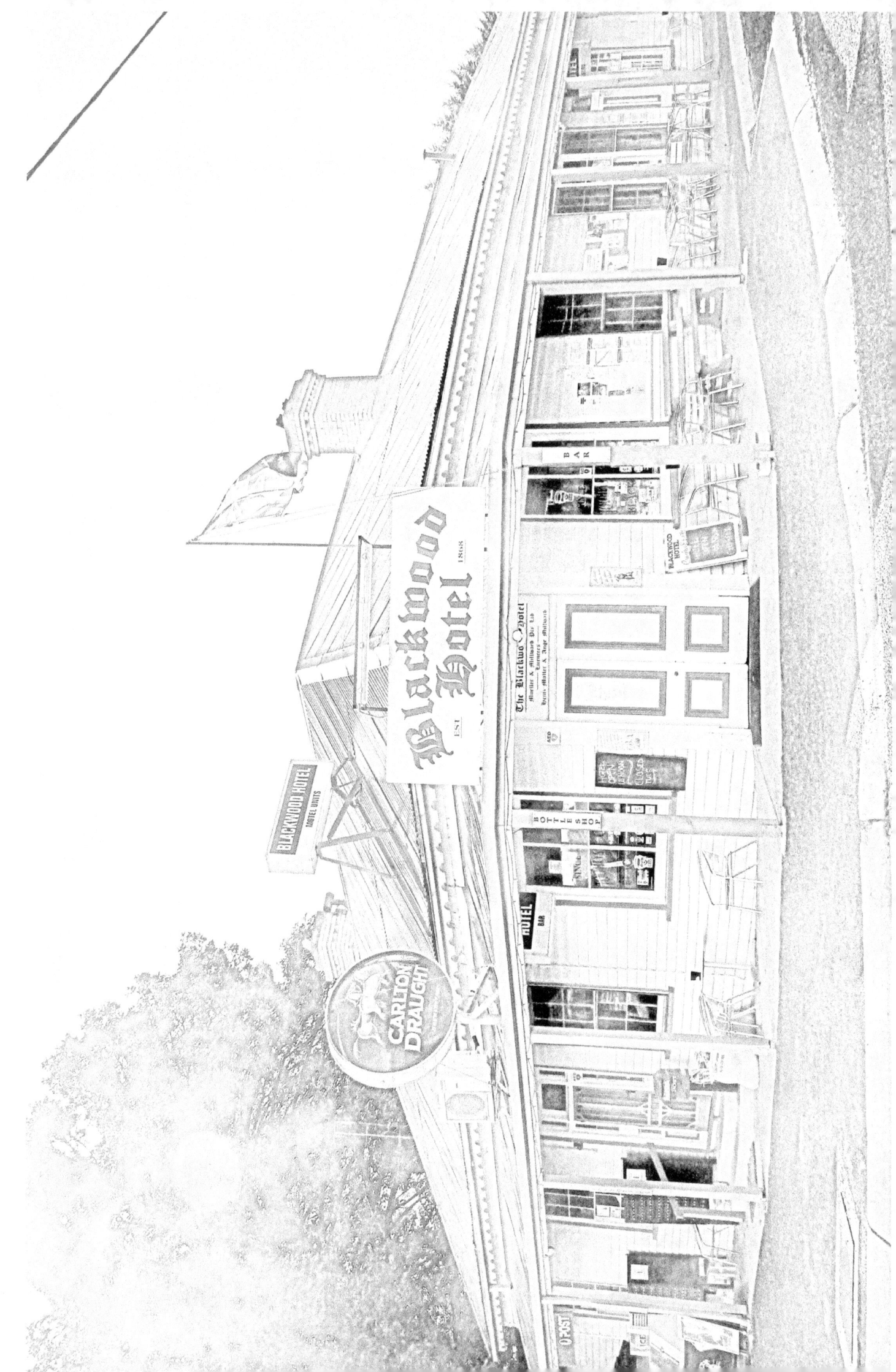

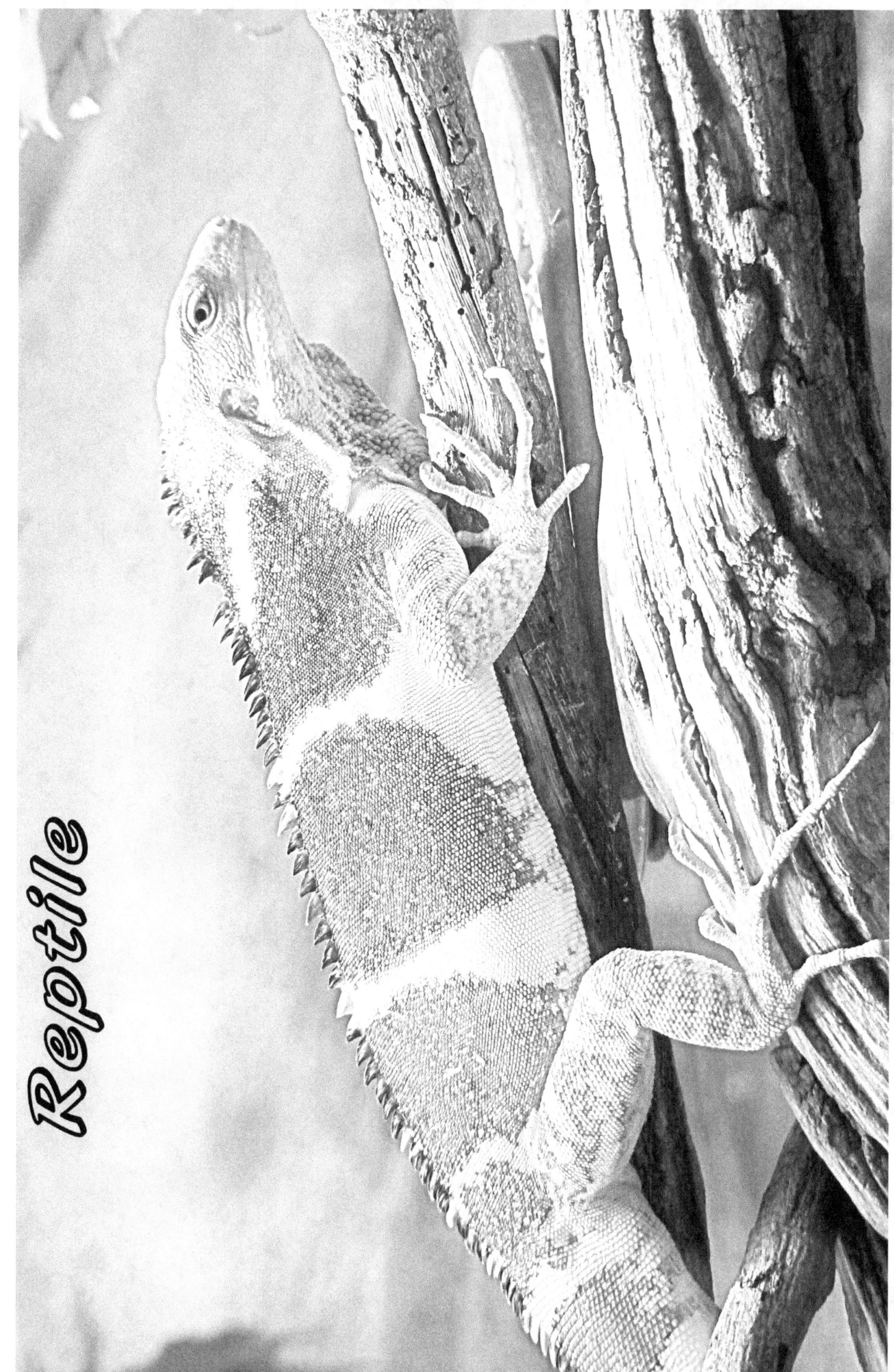

Reptile

Sailing

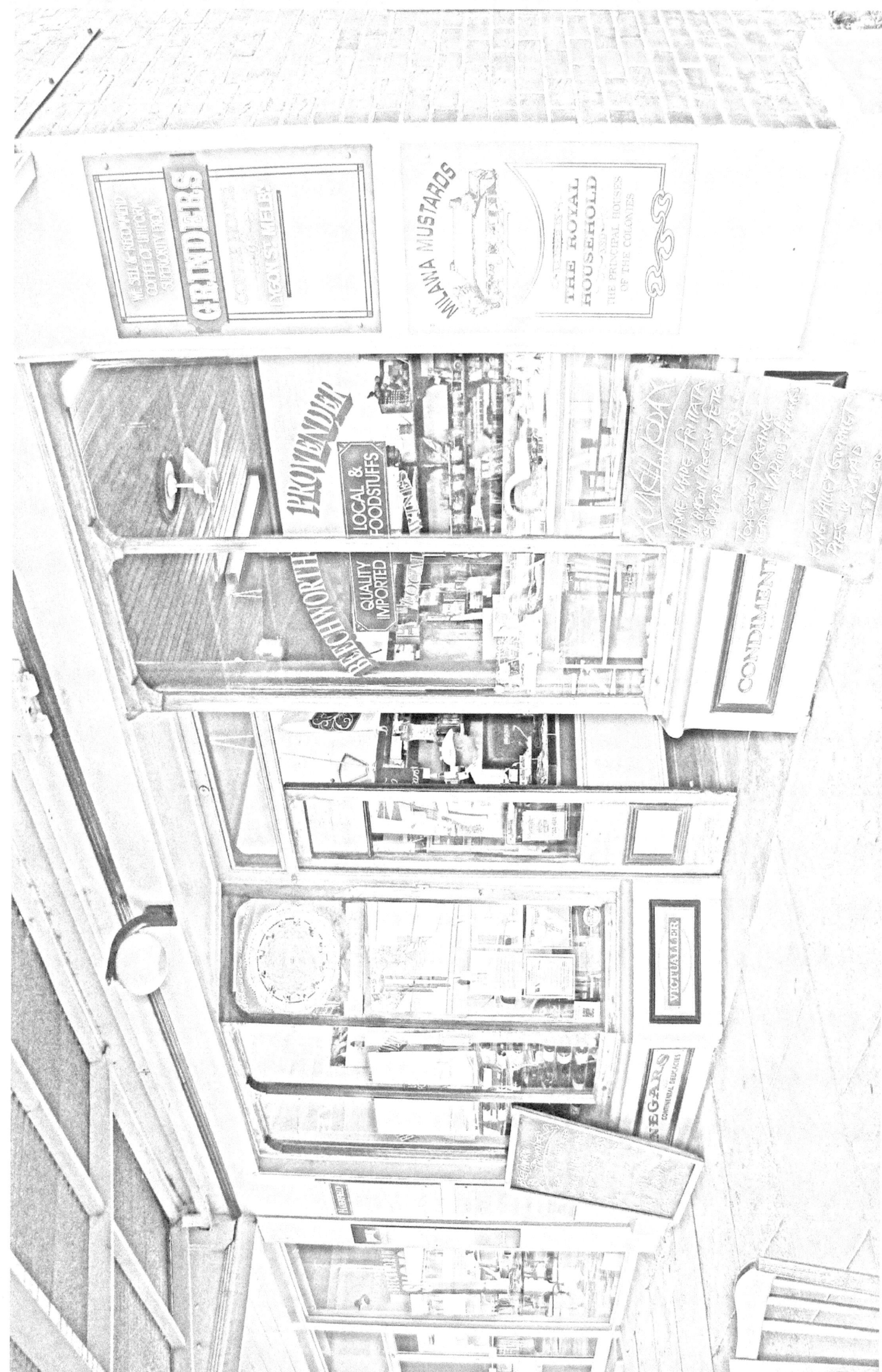

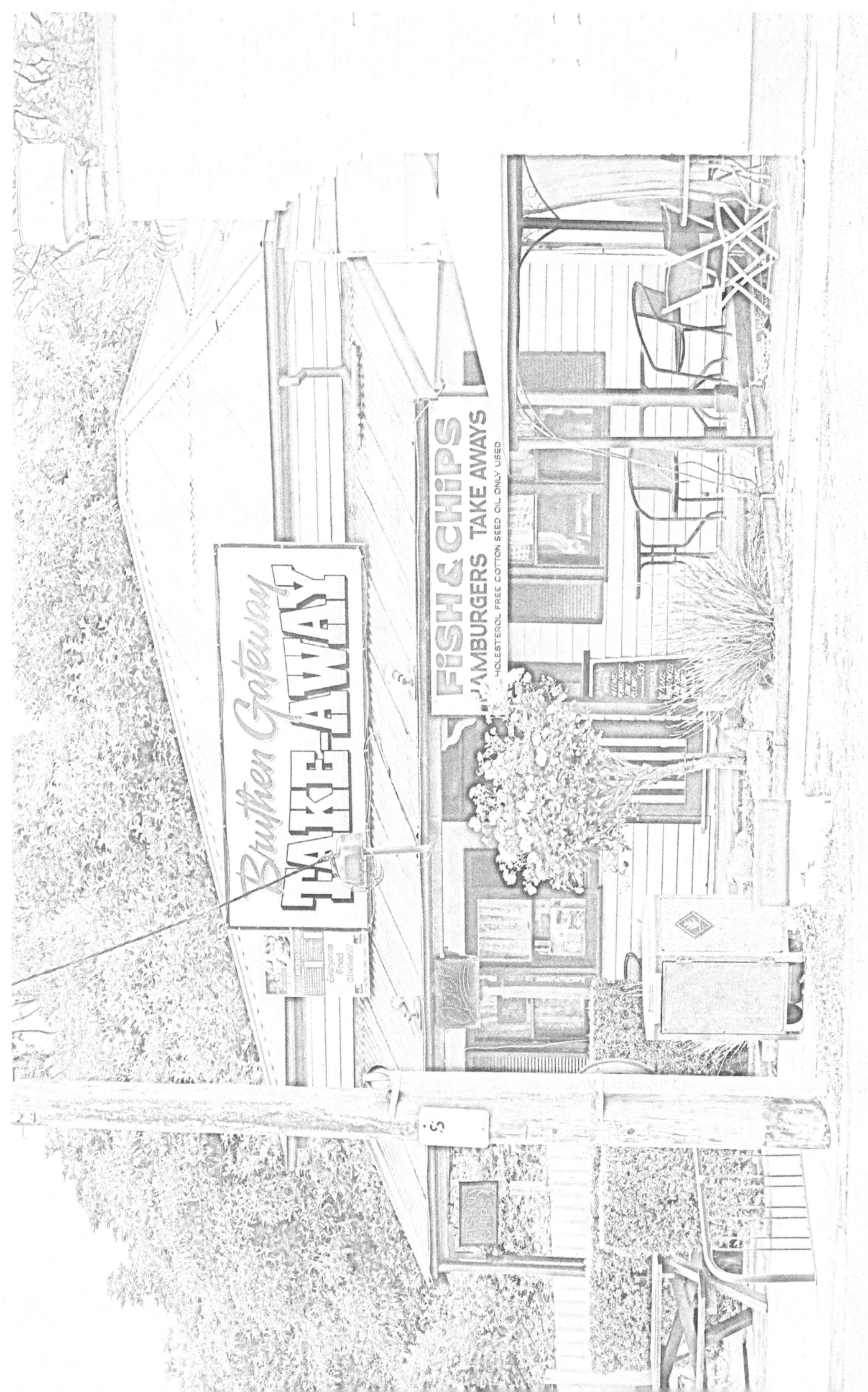

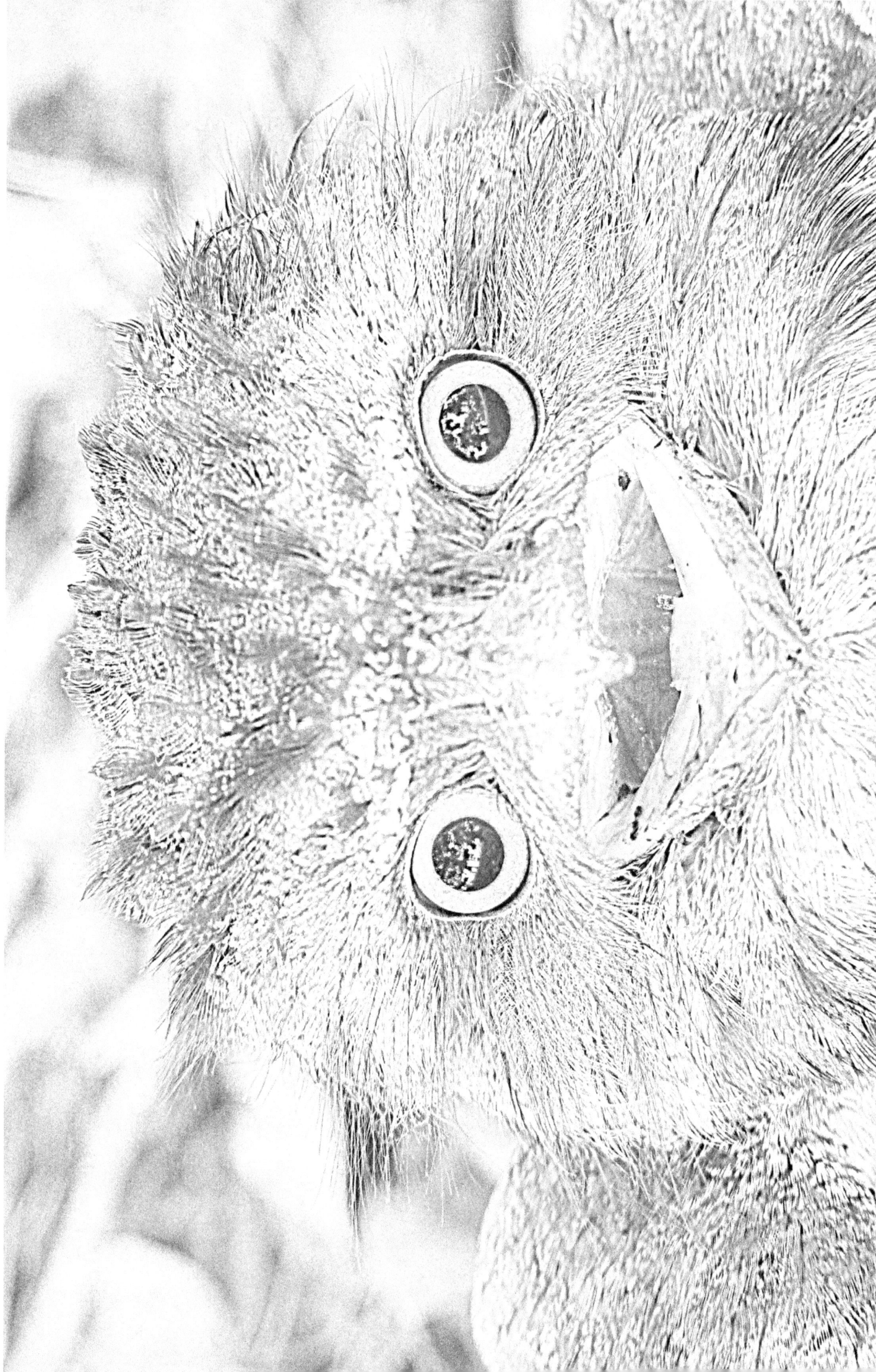

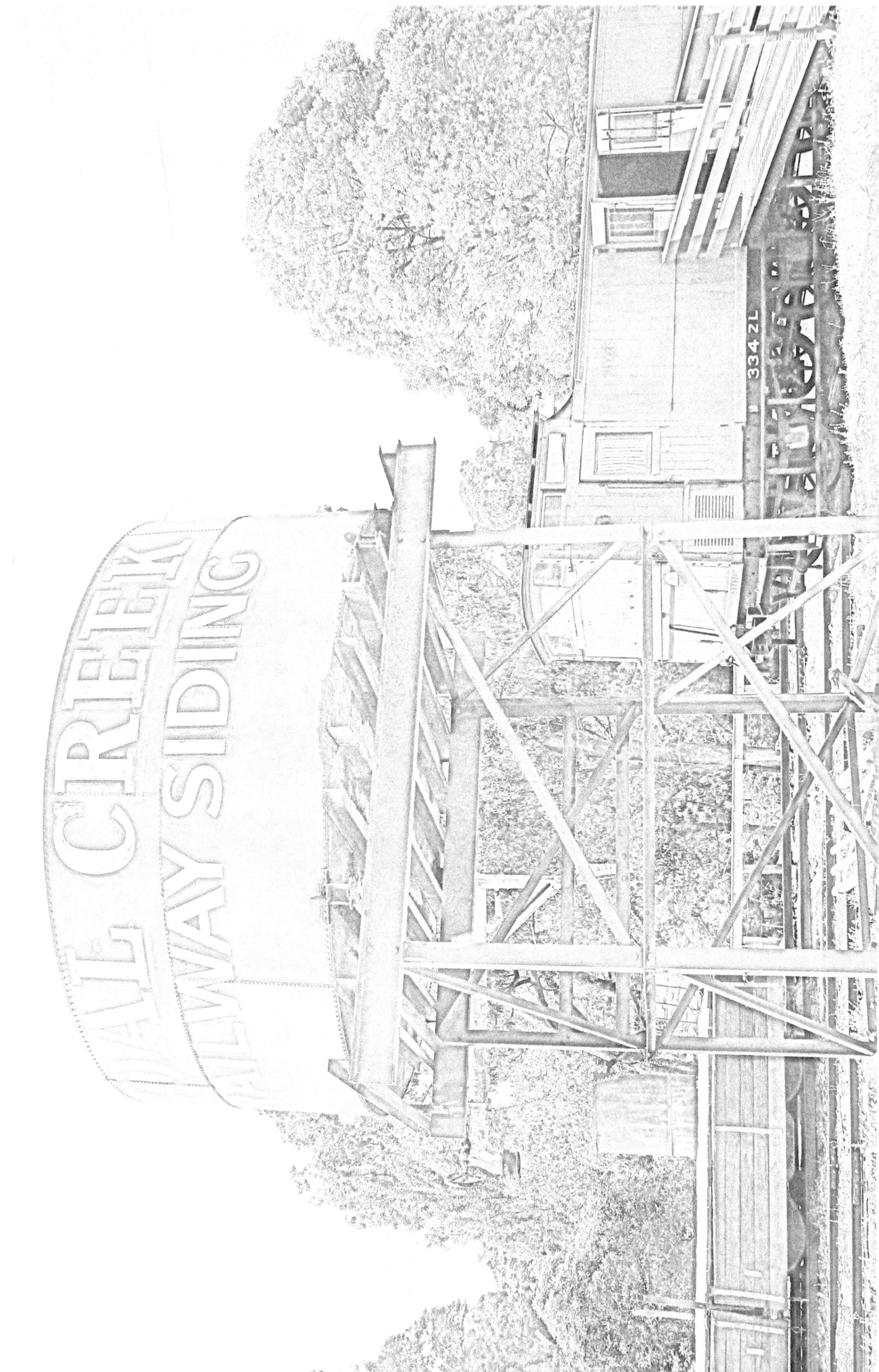

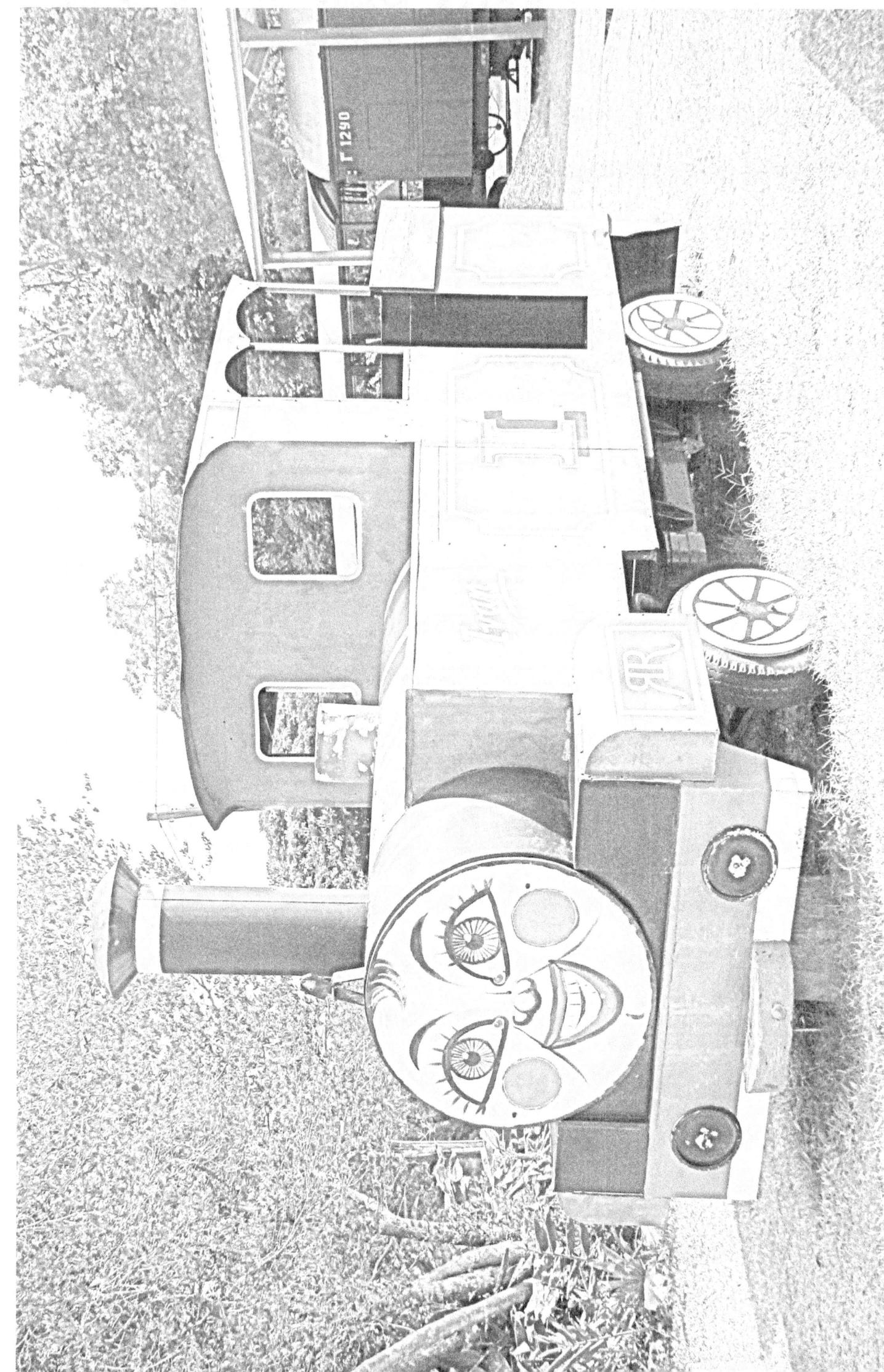

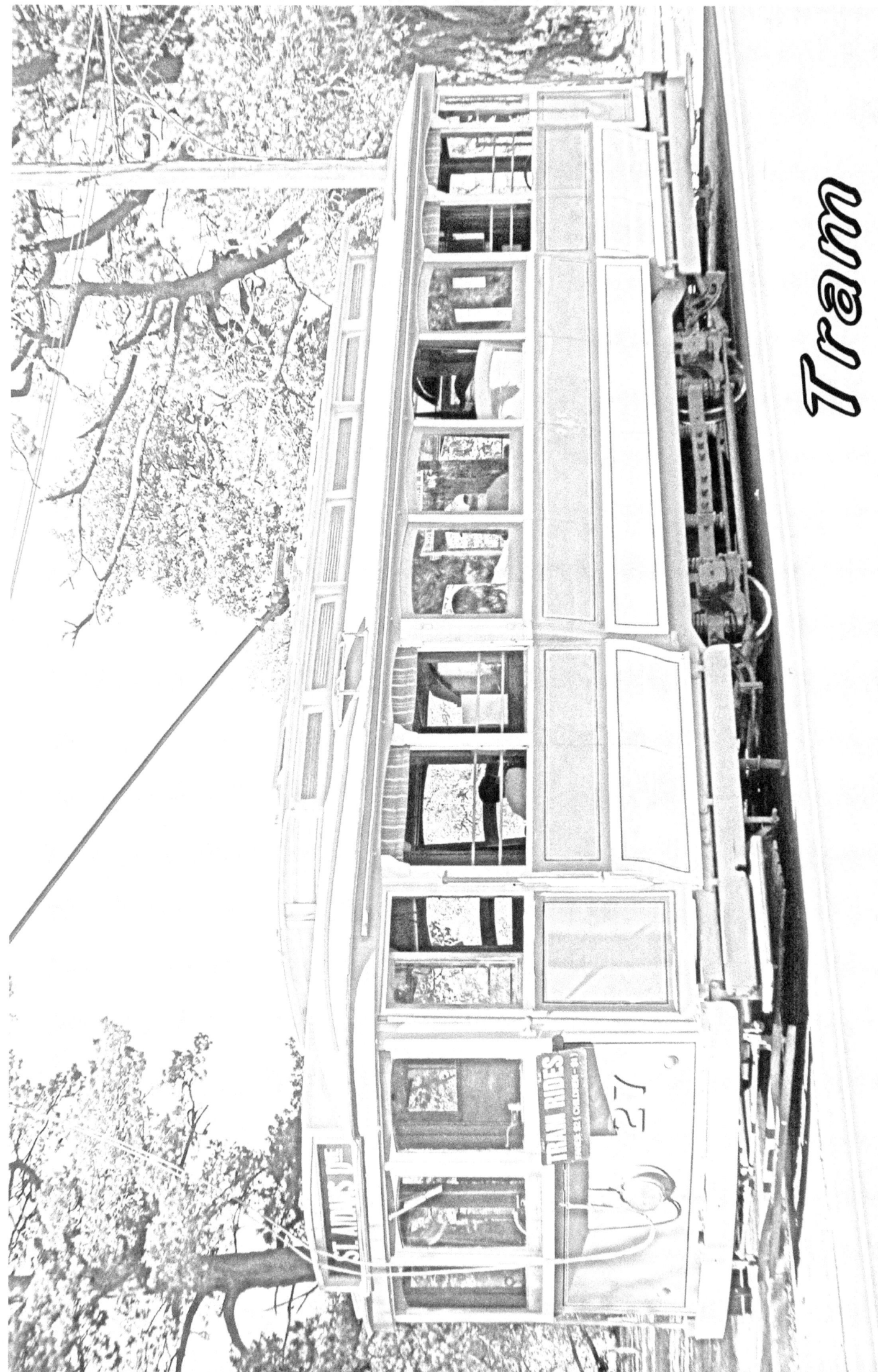

Tram

Tree Frogs

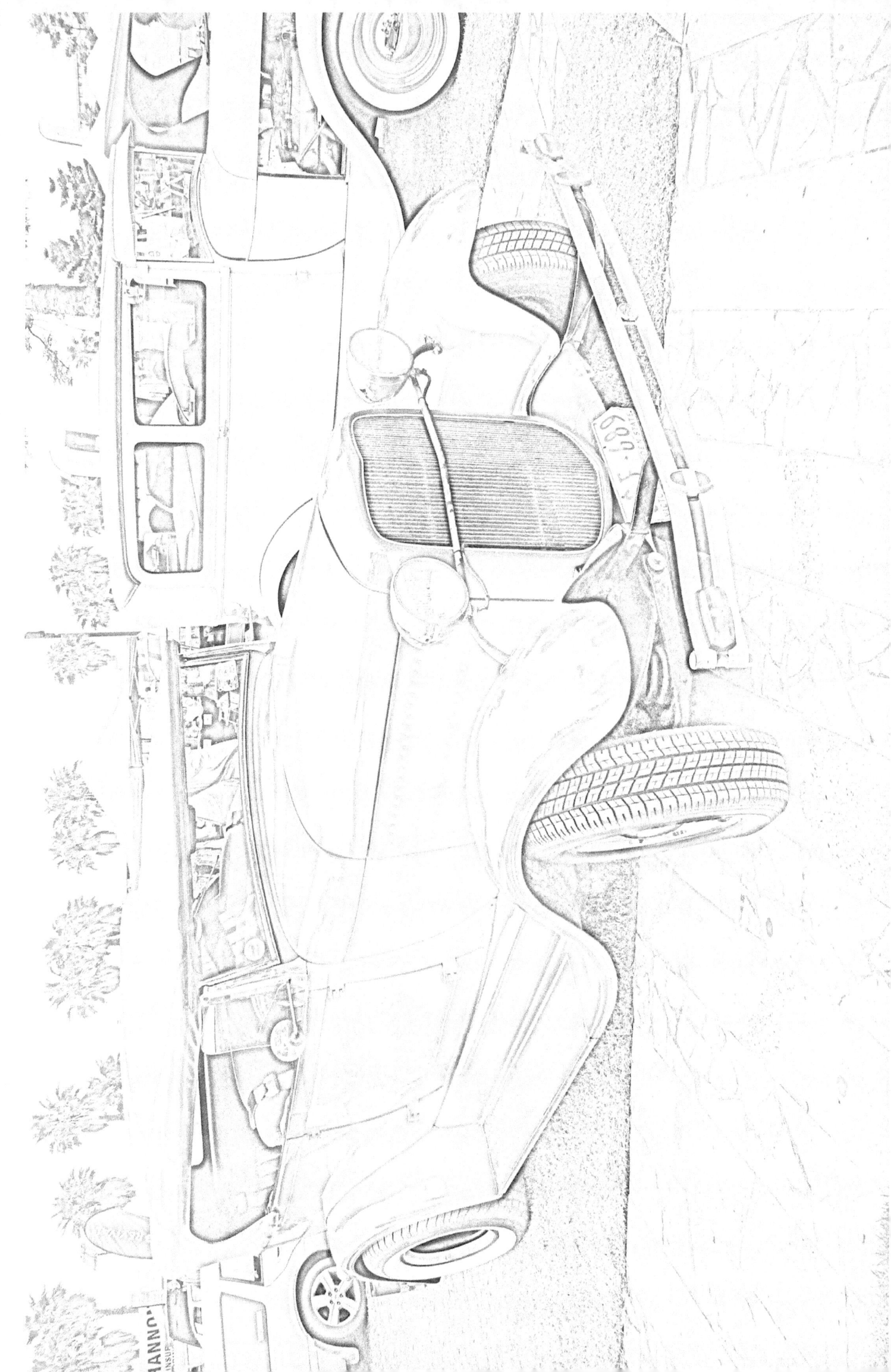

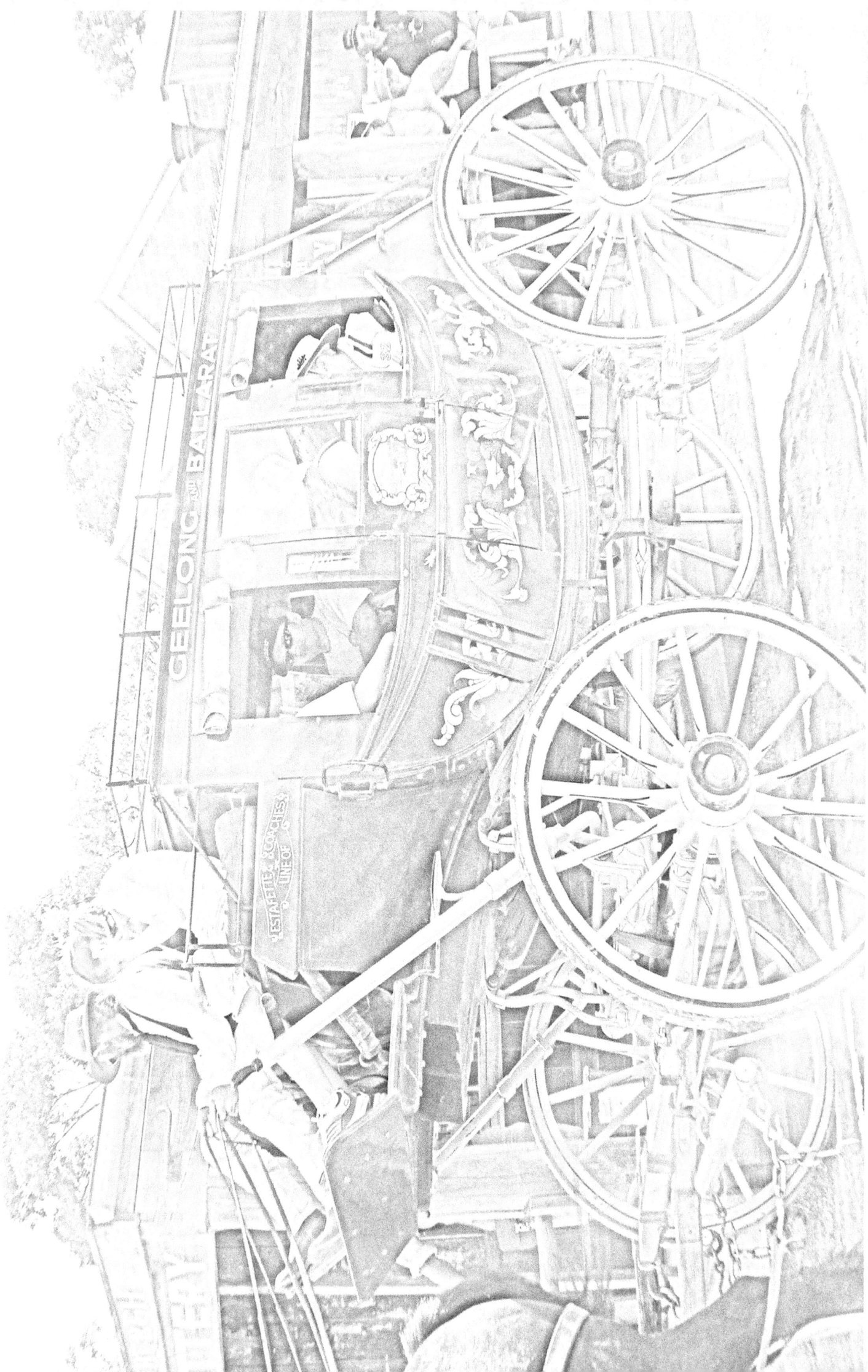

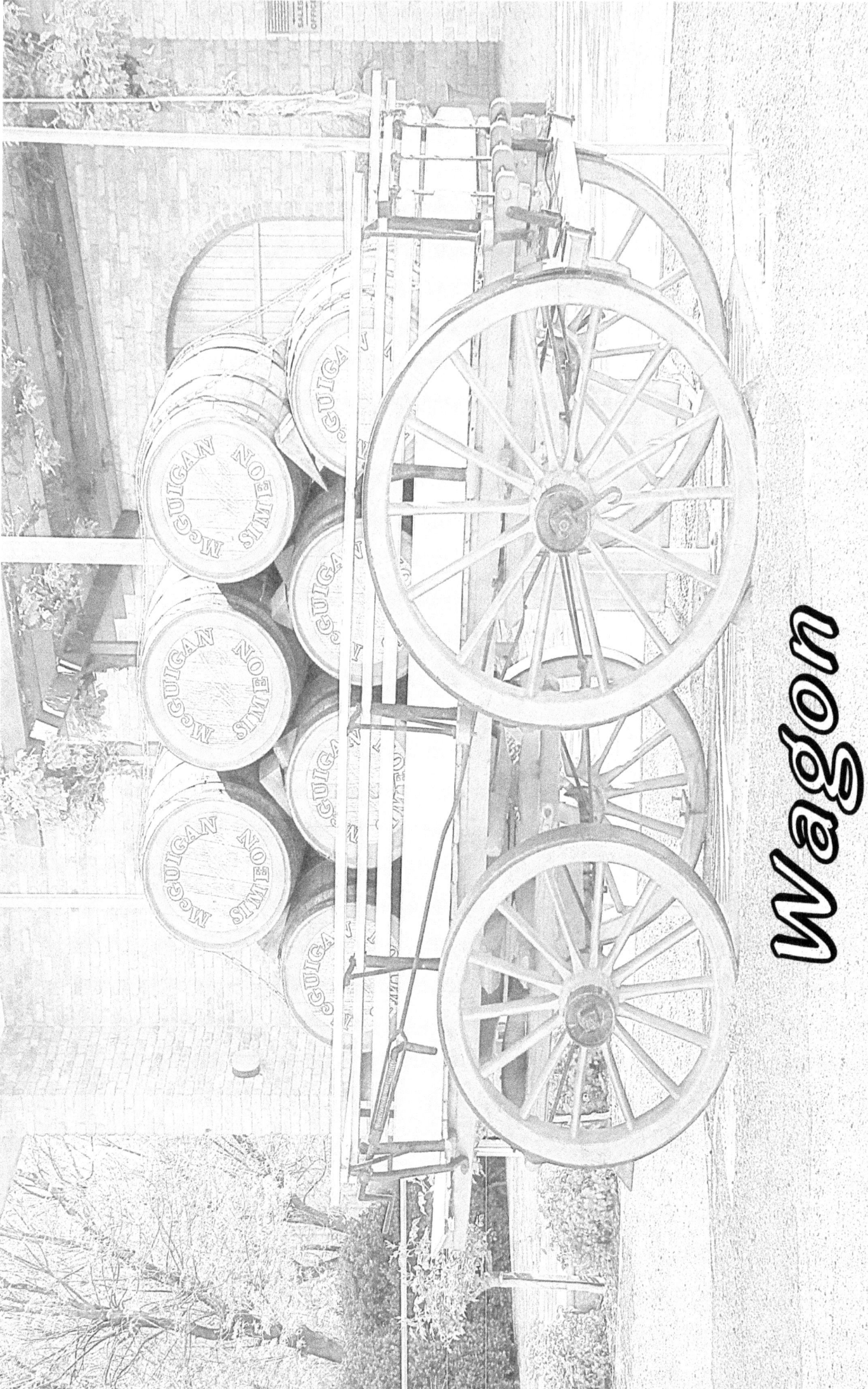

wagon

Giraffe

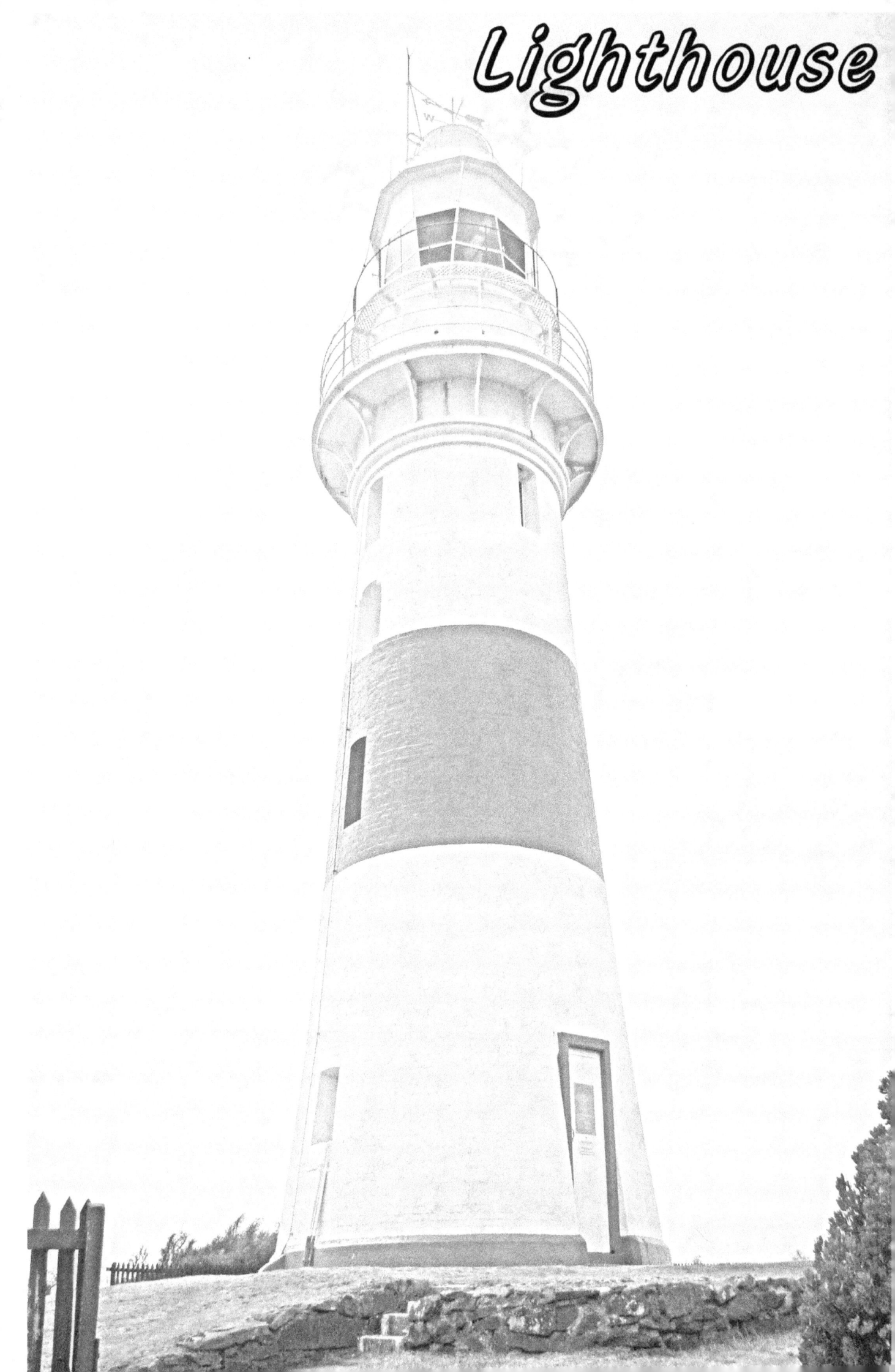

Lighthouse

Luna Park

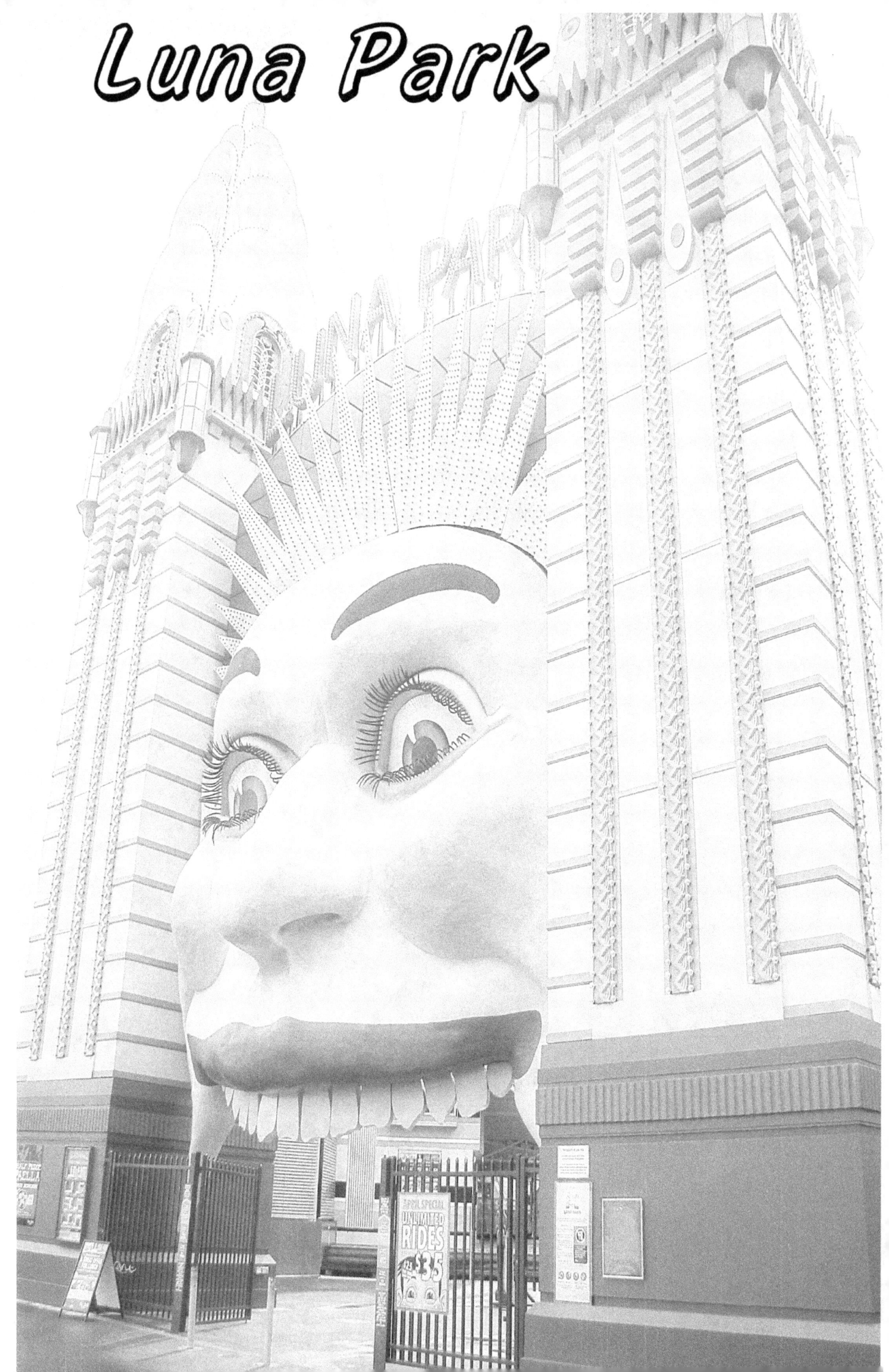

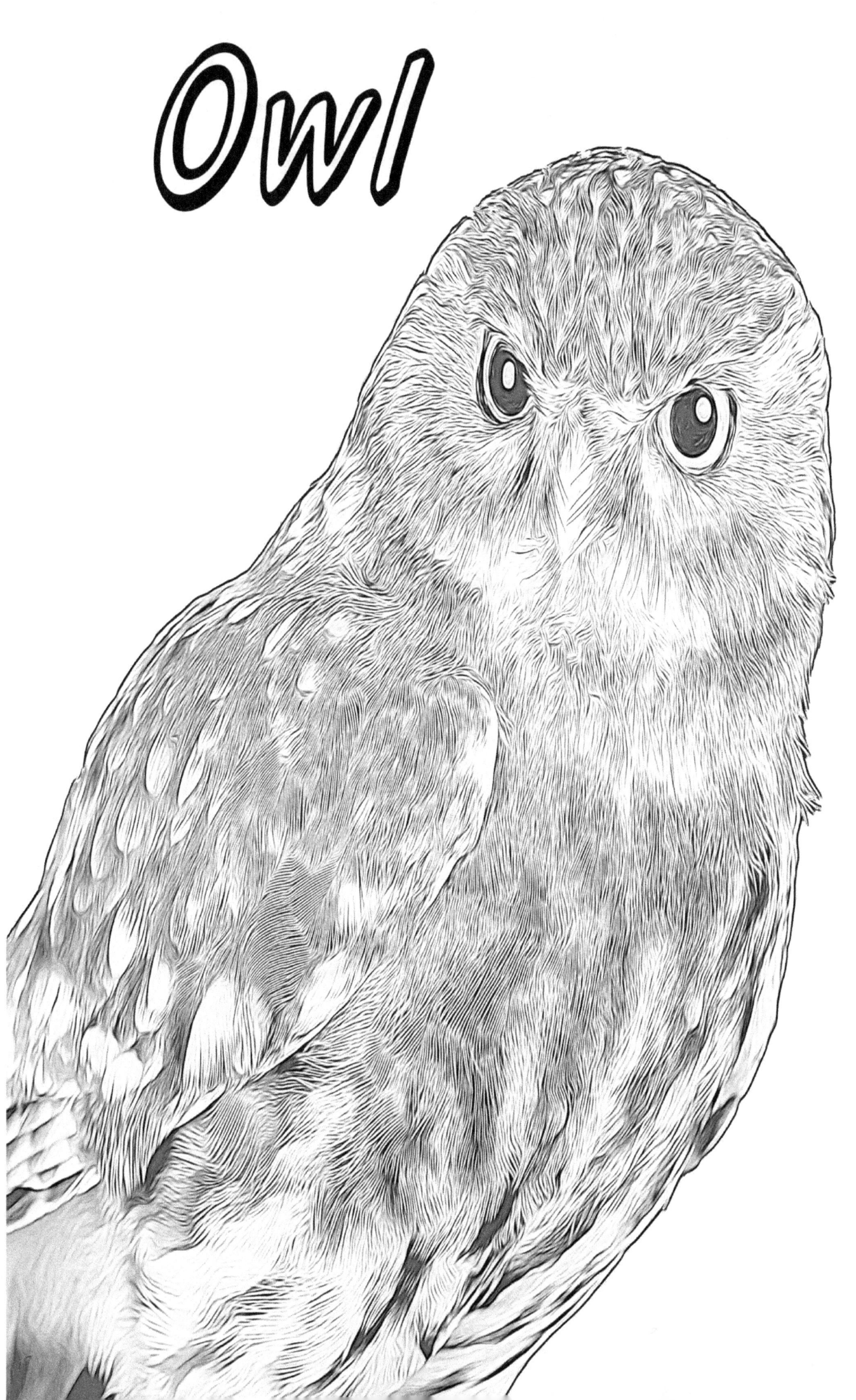

Owl

www.ingramcontent.com/pod-product-compliance
Lightning Source LLC
Chambersburg PA
CBHW081047180526
45170CB00005B/1726